Victor's Isle of Arran Adventures!

by

Victor Southgate

Amazon Publishing

First Published 2023

ISBN _____

Cover design by Irene McIntosh

Published by

Amazon

Printed by

Amazon

This book is dedicated to my daughter, son, granddaughters, grandson, and great-grandchildren with love and best wishes.

CONTENTS

ACKNOWLEDGMENTS

First, I would like to thank my family, friends, and school mates from Brodick who encouraged me to write this book after reading the stories I had submitted to the Arran Auld Photos website that people around my age could relate to. Many suggested that I write about my Arran escapades so that they could pass the stories on to their grandchildren.

I am extremely grateful to the following people for granting me permission to include their Arran photographs on the cover of my book: Jared Bowers (J. Bowers, www.VisitArran.com) for his unique panoramic photograph taken from the Brodick Castle battlement and to Fraser Aitchison for his stunning sunset photograph; and to Alasdair Hendry for permitting me to include his map of Arran from his book, *My Walks of Arran*. Also, to my parents and Aunt Elsie Pellegrini for preserving their old family photographs that were passed down enabling me to include them in my stories.

A special thanks goes to my charismatic pal, John (Hacky) Hartley, for allowing me to write about the high jinks we got up to in our early years.

My sincere appreciation goes to Jim Baguley for offering to edit the book for me. And my sincere thanks goes to Irene McIntosh for designing the book cover, photograph inserts, and reviewing the book.

I greatly appreciate all the times my granddaughter, Victoria Williamson, printed numerous book revisions for me and submitted my book for publication to Amazon. Your patience and support was a real blessing.

But most of all, my heartfelt gratitude goes to Loretta Duncan Prugh for encouraging me into undertaking writing this book. She volunteered to type it, helped me take photographs, and researched specific events relevant to stories in my book. Thank you for your participation in this two-year journey with me.

ISLE OF ARRAN MAP

Alasdair Hendry's map from his book *My Walks of Arran* May 1988

Arran has been described as "Scotland in Miniature for many years." There is certainly something mystical about Arran - if you have lived there or visited there, you will yearn to return to explore more of this fascinating island.

Chapter 1 - CASTLE CONNECTION

Isle of Arran

The Isle of Arran is a small island located in the Firth of Clyde estuary on the west coast of Scotland where a swath of wild beauty features picturesque scenery in every direction; a vast history to be discovered in the mountains, waterfalls, King's Cave, the prehistoric circle of stones and standing stones of Machrie Moor, and much more.

The changing seasons dramatically alter the landscape and views of the island. Winter's stark contrast of dramatic dark and heavy clouds to the brilliant white snow-capped mountains, the myriad of changing colours and hues brought on by spring, summer, and autumn as each season gives new vibrance to the land forming idyllic scenery such as to create an artist's or photographer's paradise.

The island is accessed via Caledonian MacBrayne (CalMac) ferries sailing every day (weather and maintenance permitting) from Ardrossan Harbour on the mainland to Brodick Pier or from Carradale on the Kintyre peninsula to Lochranza. In addition to serving the island inhabitants, the ferries are paramount in supporting the thriving tourist trade on Arran. Visitors to the island can enjoy many sport and leisure activities including hill walking, mountain climbing, pony trekking, cycling, fishing and camping. Golf enthusiasts can choose from seven scenic and challenging courses. Another attraction you may consider touring is the one brewery or the two distilleries open to visitors. Be sure to treat yourself to some 'Arran Gold,' a pleasant cream liqueur similar to Bailey's Irish Cream but much, much better in my opinion. Accommodation ranges from hotels to boarding houses, self-catering cottages to caravans, rental houses and flats.

The Castle

Brodick Castle has a long and noteworthy history. The impressive red sandstone structure sits on the side of a hill surrounded by forests overlooking a panoramic view that sweeps across Brodick Bay to Brodick Village. The majestic Goatfell Mountain peak, the highest mountain on Arran, dominates the skyline behind the castle and is quite a site to see from any view point.

The oldest part of the castle dates back to the 1200s with several alterations added to it over the centuries. In 1947 King George VI, Queen Elizabeth, Princess Elizabeth, Princess Margaret, and Phillip Mountbatten visited Arran. The Royal Family members planted four commemorative oak trees in the castle grounds that are still on display today. The well preserved castle has been a very popular tourist attraction for over 100 years.

Brodick Castle with my daughter, Carol, and son, Russell, sitting on the front steps - 12 September 2021

Jared Bowers panoramic view of Brodick Bay taken from Brodick Castle battlement N/D

Secret Passage

Brodick Castle had a secret passage close to the Wine Port Pier on the Corrie Road that went right up to the old part of the castle where a deep well was used for storing venison, pheasants, grouse, and ducks. With no refrigeration available at that time, the well was dark and cold enough to keep the game from decaying. It was the gamekeeper's job to keep it well stocked.

The castle also had a large 20 foot wooden boat with an inboard engine named the Croban for guests to make use of during the summer months. In spring the Croban was brought out of its winter home, rolled down a set of rails into Strabane Bay for summer anchorage where it would remain until being pulled back up to the boathouse by tractor for winter storage. The gamekeeper also made good use of the Croban for setting lobster pots along the Corrie shore. The Montrose family and their guests were well fed!

Wine Port Pier - 31 August 2022

Family Ties

My family connection to Brodick Castle began with my maternal grandfather, Malcolm Sillars, when he gained employment there as a castle gardener. Later, in the 1920s, my paternal grandfather, Albert Southgate, moved his family from England to Scotland to become a coachman to the Duke and Duchess of Montrose at their Buchanan Castle residence near Loch Lomond.

Lady Mary Louise Hamilton (1884-1957) was the only daughter of Scottish nobleman, William Douglas-Hamilton, 12th Duke of Hamilton (1845-1895). She inherited Brodick Castle through a trust set up by her father prior to his death in 1895.

In 1906 Lady Mary Louise married James Graham, 6th Duke of Montrose (1878-1954). He was a Scottish nobleman, naval officer, politician, and an engineer. The Duke was also credited with taking the first film of a solar eclipse of the Sun, inventor of the world's first naval aircraft carrier, and designed and owned the first seagoing heavy oil motor ship.

The Montrose family resided at Buchanan Castle until around 1925 when they changed their residential home to Brodick Castle on the Isle of Arran. My Grandfather Southgate and his family moved to Arran along with the Duke and Duchess where he continued to be their coachman. The Duke of Montrose provided my

Grandfather Southgate with a house for his family at Cladach, situated just below Brodick Castle grounds close to the sandstone Wine Port Pier on Corrie Road.

The Duke and Duchess of Montrose were both avid game hunters and saw the potential for a good source of income from renting out the living quarters of the castle to game hunters. Between the game hunting business and rent from the farms that they owned, they had a good living. When hunting parties rented the castle, the Montrose family would relocate to Dougarie Lodge during September and October. My Grandfather Southgate had the job of driving the castle children, along with all their luggage, over the String Road using the pony and trap to transport them to Dougarie Lodge on the west coast of the island.

The Duke of Montrose was instrumental in creating many jobs through his Arran Estate operations to become the biggest employer on the Isle of Arran. The Duke passed away in 1954.

In 1957 the Duchess of Montrose died and her two daughters, Lady Jean and Lady Mary, became landowners on the island. Brodick Castle, including the majority of its contents, and gardens became the property of the National Trust for Scotland in lieu of death duties.

Nineteen fifty-seven was the year I began working for Lady Jean Fforde at the Home Farm. She had a terrific sense of humour, was very kind, considerate to her employees, and always actively involved in all parts of her Arran Estate as well as the local communities.

Dougarie Lodge: Montrose family residence during hunting Season - 14 June 2022

The Castle Children

Prince Rainier III of Monaco and his sister, Princess Antoinette, would spend their summer holidays at Brodick Castle with their Montrose cousins, Lord James Angus, Lady Mary, Lord Ronald, and Lady Jean. Lady Jean was the youngest and according to my dad, Victor Southgate, the mischievous ringleader of the children from the castle.

The children loved to escape from the confines of the castle and go down to Cladach to play hide-and-seek around the sawmill and stables with the Southgate children, Victor, Elsie, Gwen, and Willie. Another favourite game they came up with was to put stones into the buckets of the big water wheel that drove the turbine to generate electricity for the castle and sawmill. I'm sure the weight of the stones must have disturbed the mechanism. The water that turned the water wheel was diverted from the Goatfell Burn and the children had great fun seeing who could make their boat, made out of wood from the sawmill yard, sail all the way down to the seashore at Strabane beach - except for the times when the nanny of the visiting Prince and Princess would appear on the scene raging at them for slipping away from the castle without permission.

My Grandfather Southgate taught the castle children to ride horses. They loved when he hitched up the pony and trap and drove them around the castle grounds entertaining them with stories or singing songs.

Grandpa Southgate with a very young Lady Jean on her pony N/D

Grandpa Southgate with Lady Jean as a young girl on her pony N/D

19

Grandpa Southgate with Prince Rainier, Princess Antoinette, and their nanny is standing behind the castle donkey N/D

Prince Rainer and Princess Antionette - circa 1929

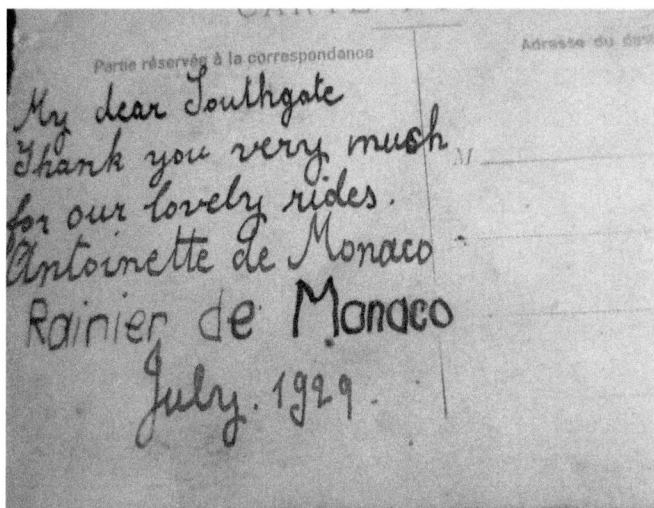

My dear Southgate
Thank you very much
for our lovely rides.
Antoinette de Monaco
Rainier de Monaco
July. 1929.

Thank you note to Grandpa Southgate written on the back of the above photograph of Prince Rainer and Princess Antionette - July 1929

The Castle Goat

The Duke of Montrose purchased Paddy the goat on the mainland for the enjoyment of the four castle children, Prince Rainer III of Monaco, Princess Antionette, and the four Southgate children. The plan was for Paddy to take the children around the castle estate in the little carriage, but he was a bit stubborn and had other ideas. Every time Paddy caught scent or sight of a favourite bush he would stop to chew on it and refuse to move. Gwen was the only one who could get Paddy to move along the path.

Gwen Southgate (my aunt) and Willie Southgate (my uncle) with Paddy the castle goat N/D

Douglas Row Houses

My mother told me that the Douglas Row houses were built in the wrong location. They should have been built at the front where the gardens are located but instead had been built against the sandstone hillside, that meant they would always be damp - and they were.

The homes were all coal fired and there were times when the wind was blowing in a certain direction that it caused a blow down of soot from the chimney that coated everything inside the house. Even the occupants would end up looking like coal men returning from working in the coal mines.

An old family photograph shows my brother, Albert, sitting with grandfather, Malcom Sillars, outside number 3 Douglas Row. Albert can still rhyme off all the family names for each of the twenty houses at Douglas Row. It was a great place to live. The large lawn at the front of the houses gave the children a great place to play outside. It was also where the men would take immense pride in maintaining their lovely gardens.

Grandpa Sillars & Albert at 3 Douglas Row N/D

Douglas Row Houses - 31 August 2022

Grandpa Sillars

Our maternal grandpa, Malcolm Sillars, spent all his life as a gardener at Brodick Castle and was the first member of our family to move into 3 Douglas Row when he became an Estate worker. Grandpa Sillars often spoke about the gardeners taking cuttings from the castle's special flowers to plant in their own gardens; giant lilies was one of their favourites. The houses were not only abundant with flower beds but also with vegetable patches and I don't believe anybody living at Douglas Row ever had to buy vegetables as all the gardens were always well stocked. The men from Douglas Row were very proud of and competitive with each other over who had the nicest garden.

The annual flower show held in Brodick Hall was a big event where it was customary for one of the castle gardeners to win most of the prizes. Brodick Castle gardens are famous for the many varieties of rhododendrons that come into bloom from April into May; a truly spectacular display in the gardens as well as all over the island. The Duchess of Montrose was also well known for her dedication in overseeing the castle gardens.

The Sillars family seems to have passed down their gardening passion to the next generation as gardening has been more than just a hobby to me for many years.

25

My cousin, John Sillars, also maintains an admirable show of flowers at his home in Brodick.

Brodick Castle Gardeners - Willie Robinson, Sr. and Grandpa Sillars N/D

Chapter 2 - GROWING UP ON ARRAN

First Up Best Dressed!

Following the Second World War in the 1940s parents had great difficulty feeding and clothing their families. It was a time of ration books for buying food and there was a lot of borrowing from each other. For most families it meant clothes being handed down from siblings. I was lucky as the clothes I inherited were my older brother's castoffs. Thank goodness he was not my sister! Shoes were also handed down and I remember giving my brother a telling off for scuffing the toes of his sandals from playing football out on the road. And talking about football, kids could play football on any road as cars were few and far between on Arran at that time.

In some of the larger families it was a case of the first one up in the morning became the best dressed for the day. I recall an incident where one young woman had been working late at one of the hotels and as she was walking home, met her youngest sister all dolled up on her way to the Saturday night dance at Brodick Hall. She immediately noticed her sister was wearing her favourite dress, so a real battle ensued between the two of them. Off came the dress right there on the shortcut path where we were playing in the field and the sister, now in her petticoat, had to go back home to start all over again.

In the late 1940s my parents, brother, and I lived in my Gran and Grandpa Sillars' small summer house located behind the main house at 3 Douglas Row. Our summer house had a corrugated iron roof and an outdoor toilet. Mum and dad slept in a bed in an alcove off of the living room. Albert and I shared a bed in a small bedroom. Bath time called for bringing out a tin bathtub while water was being boiled in a kettle over the fire. Cold water was added to get the right bath temperature, then Albert and I would take turns bathing in front of the fireplace.

I dreaded Sundays as we were not allowed to play outside. The streets were deserted. No football or golf! The women would never do a washing or hang it outside. Our Sunday routine consisted of going to church or Sunday school in the morning and then in the afternoon we would walk to Alma Terrace to visit Granny Southgate. Come Monday we were quite glad to go to school as it gave us something to do.

No ferries sailed to or from Arran on Sundays or to any of the islands on the west coast of Scotland. I remember a converted fishing boat bringing the newspapers over from the mainland every Sunday along with a priest that came over to give Sunday service at the Legion Hall near the Douglas Hotel. The priest would return to the mainland on the Monday morning ferry.

Few people who visited the island came with a car, therefore, they had to depend on the bus service scheduled to run in conjunction with the ferries docking at Brodick Pier. One bus went to the north end of the island, one to the south end, and one went over the String Road to Shiskine. As there were only two boats per day, if you missed the return bus to catch the ferry it meant you had a very long walk back to Brodick Pier.

There was also a cargo boat called *The Kildonan* that brought over all the supply goods for all of the shops on the island. *The Kildonan* also brought barrels of petrol and diesel for the garages. The barrels were decanted into underground tanks via a large funnel with fumes expelling everywhere. No health and safety criteria back in those days.

As we all grew up, we had to create our own entertainment. Vandalism was unheard of as everyone knew everybody in the village. We were all scared that our dads would hear about any mischief we may get involved in. Off would come the father's trouser belt to give a whack across the backside of their respective wayward child. It didn't do me any harm!

Even the headmasters and teachers at the primary and secondary schools enforced corporal punishment by having an errant pupil hold their arms stretched straight out, the back of one hand placed in the palm of the other, then the open upper palm would be struck with a leather strap for as many times the disciplinarian decided was fitting punishment for whatever misbehaviour had been committed. Having your knuckles rapped with a wooden ruler was another punishment and then there was the flying wooden chalkboard eraser that did not always hit the right target. Ouch! Today, none of this is allowed.

The less physical form of discipline used by teachers and school prefects (student hall monitors) at Lamlash Secondary School was to assign you to write 100 - 200 or more times, "I will not talk in class" or "I will not run in the hallway" or other text befitting the misdemeanor. We did come up with a rather creative way to speed this assignment up by holding two pencils in the one hand to write out whatever statement we were given. Parents and pupils accepted all these methods of discipline without question.

For years the only dentist on the island had a surgery in his home in Brodick as well as one at Lamlash School. He had come to the island to retire but, regrettably, that did not happen and instead he became the dreaded dentist. Pupils were lined up in their classroom then marched single file down the corridor to sit on a wooden bench right outside his dental surgery door where many waited with great trepidation to go in for their examination. Unfortunately, those waiting for treatment were subjected to seeing their peers, who just had teeth extracted, seated on another wooden bench in the same corridor where galvanized buckets filled with disinfectant were lined up in preparation for anyone that became sick from having gas anaesthetic from a dental procedure. I can still remember the smell of rubber from the gas mask. We were also subjected to hearing pupils crying from inside his surgery, not only in the corridor but also in a classroom that was right next to his surgery. Not a good thing to see or hear - a bit barbaric!

We have Jerry Lane, the very personable school janitor, to thank for suggesting to Mr. Petrie, the headmaster, that pupils recovering from gas extractions be moved into the nearby gym dressing room, across from the dental surgery, instead of being seated out in the corridor where students changing classes were also exposed to this unpleasant sight.

The Local Shop

When my dad was the manager of Curries, the largest shop on the island, he, along with Bertie Thom and Alec Sillars (Balmore) manned the counter. They were all good pals that worked well together and were great at cheering up their customers. There was no self-service, therefore, the staff had to walk back and forth to the rear of the shop for whatever a customer requested. Everything came in bulk, even the sugar came in big paper bags. They must have walked miles every day filling orders. Ivor Muir drove the delivery van and later John Corbett took over as the driver. The three men at the counter were always joking with someone. It was said that if any of the locals were feeling a bit down, they would go to Curries for their messages and leave sore from laughing. On arriving home they would discover that they had only bought half of what they had meant to pick up at the shop.

Loose-leaf tea was delivered in big wooden boxes lined with silver paper to keep the tea dry. Looking for something to do one day my pal, John Innes, and I nicked a tea box from Curries to use in an experiment to see if we could turn it into a boat. To our surprise our tea box boat did actually float and two triumphant wee boys launched it at high tide into the lagoon next to the Brodick golf course resulting in a successful maiden voyage.

During the winter months in the 1960s the tearoom above the shop became a youth club meeting place for rock and roll dances, playing badminton, table tennis and darts.

Better Than Nardinis!

Meet the famous Pellegrini ice cream family wedding party - L-R back row Granny Pellegrini, unknown, Father Pellegrini, Granny Southgate, and my dad, Victor; front row Gwen Snelgrove, Ernie & Elsie Pellegrini, and Ugo Pellegrini. N/D

Old father Pellegrini came to Arran as a First World War evacuee and the family became famous for their Brodick Cafe ice cream recipe. Aunt Elsie worked in the ice cream hut at Brodick Pier. They had another ice cream hut at the Brodick putting green and Ugo ran the Lamlash Pier Cafe selling the same famous ice cream. Cyril delivered ice cream in bulk to hotels in the cafe van. He also peddled a three-wheeler ice cream cart around the village as far as Douglas Row where the kids there made a game of pushing him around in his cart and he would reward them with a free ice cream cone.

When my dad retired from Curries shop, he went to work for his brother-in-law, Ernie, in the Brodick Cafe. He worked there for years - well into his seventies. He was the tall man in the white coat serving at the counter.

According to my dad, Ernie was the ice cream maker and when the *Waverley* paddle steamer was due to arrive at Brodick Pier, Ernie would dash to the back of the cafe to make a big batch of ice cream for the tourists. Many times it was said that Pellegrini's ice cream was better than Nardinis in Largs on the mainland. Everyone who tasted Pellegrini ice cream absolutely loved it!

The *Waverley*, built in 1946, continues to the present day making trips around the West Coast of Scotland during summer months stopping at many piers along the River Clyde where ice-cream can still be bought, but sadly not Pelligrini's.

And then there were three!

Nancy and Bobby Bell were the proud parents of the first set of triplets, Jimmy, Bobby, and Billy, to be born on the Isle of Arran and they also lived at Douglas Row.

A photo of me with the triplets in their pram - looks like one of the weans is missing but if you look closely, you can see that there are two wee faces on the left. N/D

Here I am with two of the triplets in a photograph taken behind their Gran McSkimming's house at Douglas Row. N/D

No social media in those days!

Growing up on Arran during the 1940s and 1950s was a time when very few people had televisions or telephones and anyone who did happen to have a telephone had to share it on what was known as a party line. If the other 'party' that shared your line was using their phone, you were privy to their conversation when you tried to make a call. I am sure there were many interesting conversations to be heard and a great deal of earwigging perhaps? Any messages that could not be handled by phone were communicated by telegram. I remember seeing Roy Dickey, the local postman, on his bike delivering telegrams.

In the evenings we were all accustomed to going everywhere in the dark in the wintertime. At this time of year it would start to get dark around 4:30 p.m. and there were very few streetlights to be found around Brodick. The villages of Lamlash and Whiting Bay were the same. The Power Station for the whole island was sited at Brodick Pier where the bus garage is located nowadays. The power for the island was generated using diesel. The old power station kept running until an underwater cable was installed that came across from the Mull of Kintyre on the mainland to Machrie shore.

High Jinx at the Bakery

My usual group of friends consisted of: John (Hacky) Hartley, a tall, lean, affable rascal who was always loads of fun; Toby Sillars, my cousin, a small guy with a ruddy complexion; and Roy Mullen, the quiet spoken, handsome one who became the first in our group to start smoking. Our gang number was later increased by one; a thin, pale, ginger haired boy named Sandy Grieve. His family moved to the island from Glasgow when his father secured the position of Head Baker at Wooley's Bakery. Sandy's family was the first among us to have a television. So, on winter nights when we could find nothing better to do, we would descend on Sandy's house to watch television. We would knock on the door and ask Sandy to come out to play, knowing full well he would invite us in, especially on nights when the rain was pelting down.

When the TV programs were not that great, we would slip out his house to go and play in the adjoining bakery. It was always nice and warm in there. If the locals only knew what we got up to in the bakery, they would have had a fit. We would stick our hands into the dough mixture to make figurines and when we were finished with our creations … the dough was added back into the mixture where it would become the next days bread and rolls. There was a huge tub for mixing dough that we would lift the lid to climb into (with our shoes on) when it was empty, as it made a great army tank when we played soldiers. The tub had an inspection lid that made a great look out turret for our war games.

We knew about the cage where all the goodies were stored. There was treacle, syrup, cherries, currents, raisins, and delicious fondant. The cage was always locked but Sandy knew where the key was kept and in we would go to help ourselves. Sandy would say, "Don't make it too obvious. You can take some cherries and some fondant." One time I had just stuck my hand into the fondant tub when Sandy's dad came in to check the temperature of an oven and then he left. Lucky for me the 'goodies' cage was in a corner of the bakery where Mr. Grieve could not see me quickly shove a handful of sticky fondant into my pocket. What a mess! However, at school the next day I thoroughly enjoyed eating the now hardened fondant from inside my trouser pocket. It was lovely!

Beached Whale

In school we heard about a dead whale being discovered on Brodick beach so the boys were eager to get out of school that day to go down to the beach to get a close look at this fascinating find. We ended up playing on it. One of the boys started to cut his initials into the whale's body with his pen knife just as a woman was walking her dog along the beach and she gave him hell for desecrating the dead animal. We were playing on the whale when the headman from the council arrived to decide on a course of action on how to dispose of it.

The next day we watched Johnny Henderson, the boat hirer, attach a rope to the whale's tail and drag it down to the water's edge with his tractor at high tide. Two crewmen from the puffer coal boat rowed a small boat in to the beach to pick up the rope from Johnny, then they returned to the puffer where the rope was attached to the boat winch to enable them to pull the whale out into deeper water. We witnessed the carcass being towed out to sea to be blown up with dynamite - never to be seen again.

Brodick Pier

The Brodick boys spent a lot of time hanging out at Brodick Pier amusing themselves fishing. We would fish under the pier looking for all sorts of items that had fallen from ferry passengers' pockets. This was at a time when most men carried cigarette cases inside their jacket pockets and when they would lean over the ferry railing, the cigarette case would fall into the sea just waiting to be discovered.

We had quite an ingenious way of retrieving objects from under the pier. A fishing line would be dropped down close to a big starfish for it to grab onto then it was pulled up to the surface where a fishing hook was inserted into its back. The starfish was then lowered down onto a cigarette case or whatever we were after. Once the starfish made contact with the item, the suckers would latch on allowing us to pull our prize out of the water, making us very chuffed with our successful achievement. One of the things I retrieved using this technique was a watch with a broken strap.

The pier was always a great source of entertainment and none more so than watching motorists trying to navigate the tricky maneuvers required to drive their cars off the *Glen Sannox* open deck utilizing two wooden planks for a gangway to disembark vehicles onto the pier. A number of times the drivers gave up through sheer panic and requested a crew member drive their car off the ferry. I specifically remember a Ford Zephyr Zodiac, a lovely car, that slipped off the planks and ripped the exhaust pipe clean off. First stop was the pier garage for repairs.

Hacky, Toby and I also liked going down to Brodick Pier when the puffer coal boat came in to watch them off-load the coal into lorries. We would ask the drivers if we could go with them to deliver the coal. Sometimes we would be lucky and get a run to Lochranza which was a very long distance away to us. It seemed like the other side of the world instead of just the other side of the island.

Another good run we enjoyed was to Blackwaterfoot as that was also considered to be a long drive. When the drivers did allow us to go with them, it gave us the opportunity to explore the island and have fun at the same time. It is perhaps worth mentioning at this point that the A841 Road, which goes around the perimeter of the island, is a mere 56 miles round trip.

Lochranza Castle - 14 June 2022

Water Pistols

One sunny summer day my pals and I decided to spend the day at Brodick beach. We had played all the games we could think of and even had a football match with the locals against the visitors. When the game was over, one of the visitors produced a big water pistol and soaked all of us.

This became a new challenge for the local boys. We ran up to Alexander's shop across from the beach and helped ourselves to water pistols from a big tub that sat outside the front door of the shop. As nobody had any money, we decided to just borrow them and bring them back when we had finished playing with them.

We ended up having a water pistol fight among ourselves. Great fun! And yes we did return the water pistols to the shop undamaged. But there was only one problem, Hacky's water pistol did not work very well so he went into the shop to complain about it - and he was reimbursed. What a charmer he was!

We could not believe our luck!

My brother and I started playing golf at an early age when we lived at Douglas Row in the field we called 'the shortcut' where Montrose House was eventually built. We played against our neighbours, John and Colin Innes. As we did not have the luxury of playing golf with real golf clubs, we started off using a walking stick with a crook handle and a tennis ball for a golf ball. We would practice for hours at a time until there was a winning team, all the while trying to dodge the coo pats in the field.

We could not believe our luck on the day that Albert happened to be riding his bike past 17 Douglas Row just as Mrs. Armit was about to throw a set of hickory golf clubs into the bin, but instead she offered them to him. They had belonged to her deceased husband who had been the greenskeeper at the Brodick Golf Club. Albert gave me the odd numbered clubs and he kept the even numbers ... now we could head for the Brodick golf course which was only about 200 yards away from our house and play with real clubs.

Kids were not allowed on the golf course unless they had an adult with them. The older club members did not give us any encouragement whatsoever to take up golf, unlike today with kids getting tuition throughout the summer holidays. I know that Hacky as well as Russell Duncan, a hotel owner and also a dedicated golfer, have spent countless hours teaching and encouraging kids to play golf for many years. As a club member, Russell became very protective of the golf course when it became jeopardized due to erosion caused as a result of sand extraction from the Brodick and Strabane beaches that border some sections of the golf course.

As we were teaching ourselves to play golf on the course, if we spotted golfers coming towards us when we were out practicing our game, we would hide in the bushes until they had passed, then we would continue playing another few shots until the next group of golfers came along. We became very speedy players on the Strabane holes 9, 10, 11, 12 and 13, because this area was out of sight of the Club House. On hot summer evenings a lot of adult golfers would play the 8th green and jump to the 14th tee if the midges were making it too miserable to play the whole course (that meant they were skipping the Strabane section of the course that we liked to play on).

The Brodick Golf Club had a strict rule in the 1950s of no golfing on a Sunday while the Brodick Church service was being held as the first three holes of the course were in Ormadale Park which was directly across from the church.

Also, in the late 1950s the club held a 'long drive' competition during the summer that the visitors looked forward to participating in just as much as the locals. John Innes and I were stationed beside the second fence at the fourth hole, as it was then, where it was our job to retrieve the golf balls and measure the longest drive distance for David Middleton to record the golfer's score. When my uncle, Ernie Pellegrini, was taking his shot in the contest, he hooked his drive. His golf ball hit the main road, bounced off and hit the front door of the St. Elmo Hotel just as a visitor was coming out the door. This competition was great fun for all the participants.

Another amusing golf competition was between professional archer, George Hamilton, and one of the Brodick Club's best golfers. A target was placed behind each of the courses 18 holes for the archer to aim at while the golfer played his normal game. I remember the archer's arrowhead sticking into an old hawthorn tree at the 10th hole target where the arrow shaft broke on impact. I think the archer won and the locals and visitors enjoyed this unusual entertainment.

Golfers had to play across the Rosaburn that flowed out to Brodick Bay. When the tide went out, we would wade into the burn to recover players' lost golf balls and keep them for ourselves. All good fun and we were lucky

47

enough to evade ever being caught playing golf in the Strabane area.

The four of us ended up being really good golfers. Albert and Colin paired up as locals to play against the visitors and they never lost a match. Albert, went on to become a professional golfer in Scotland and in Canada. I held a one handicap for over 30 years and an eight handicap in my 80th year. The Innes brothers were also excellent low handicap golfers. Our fierce competitiveness at an early age set us all up for a life-long future of enjoyment playing golf. Not too bad for starting out with a walking stick and a tennis ball! As of April 2023, Albert and I have each achieved 11 holes in one during our long golfing careers.

Two other family members were also excellent golfers. My mum, Margaret Southgate, was the recipient of the *Brodick Ladies Golf Club Trophy* in 1959 and was a Captain in 1960. Aunt Elsie (Southgate) Pellegrini received *The Brodick Ladies' Golf Club Trophy* in 1936 and 1974. She also held the title of Brodick Ladies Captain in 1937, 1950 and 1962.

When the Brodick Golf Club celebrated its first century of golf in 1997, Aunt Elsie was recognised as the longest serving member and granted the honour of unveiling the Centenary Sundial at the opening ceremony.

L-R Aunt Elsie, Margaret Gold, Russell Duncan and Willie Innes at the Unveiling of the Centenary Sundial - 15 March 1997

As a golf professional in Canada my brother had the unique experience of providing golf lessons to two very dedicated celebrity golfers. Bob Hope the comedian and film star, as well as Alice Cooper the singer, songwriter, and actor.

L-R Albert with Bob Hope circa 1986

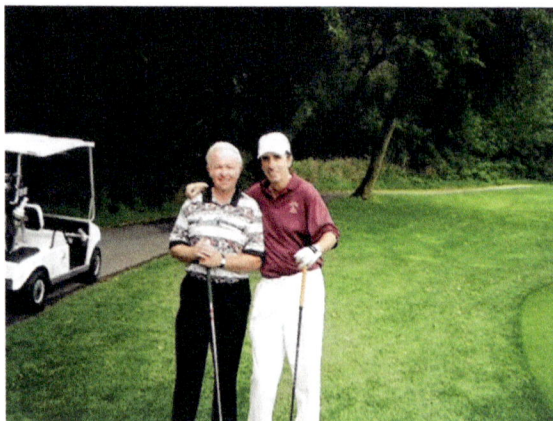

L-R Albert with Alice Cooper circa 1995

Myself, Archie, and Hugh Hamilton N/D

Jamboree

Haven't we scrubbed up well! Here I am with my next door neighbours, Archie and Hugh Hamilton, at Springbank Terrace just before we left for the Jamboree being held at the Lamlash Church. I can't recall what the parade was about. Local Brownies, Girl Guides, Cubs, Scouts, and Boys Brigade organizations attended including groups from the mainland.

The Boys Brigade

Boys had the opportunity to join the Boys Brigade when we attended Brodick Primary School. Mr. Needle, a Lamlash Secondary School geography teacher, was the Captain of our Boys Brigade group. He was short, balding, heavy built, wore thick lens glasses and was renowned for his strictness. When he was giving someone a telling off tiny droplets of saliva would spray from his mouth.

During a jamboree we had with a Boys Brigade group from Glasgow, Mr. Needle arranged for us to invite the Glasgow boys to come for a weekend stay at our homes on Arran. They then reciprocated by inviting us to stay with them at their homes in Glasgow. The boys from Glasgow enjoyed Arran so much that the following year the whole group came back to camp in Glen Rosa and continued to do so for many years after that.

Run!

Heading home from the Boys Brigade meetings was an ideal opportunity for us lads to get up to more mischief and playing 'chap and run' was one of our regular pranks. This game involved us chapping a door and running as fast as we could before the owner opened the door to spot us. Our favourite door to chap belonged to Jim Alexander who lived down the lane leading to Alexander's Houseware shop. He was a heavy-set man with a good sense of humour and knew what time we would be passing by his house. Jim would be waiting at the back of his door with his running gear on ready to chase us along the road to the Pellegrini Cafe shortcut footpath that takes you up to Alma Road. We were young, fit and able to run up the cafe shortcut faster than Jim - easily making our escape.

Also, on our walk home from the Boys Brigade, we passed Tigh-na-Mara on the main road where two doors were right next to one another belonging to two different home owners. This was just too good an opportunity for us to resist, so we would tie the two door handles together with string, chap the two doors then run and hide across the road in the bushes. We would laugh ourselves silly watching the fun as each occupant tried in vain to open their door in a mini tug-o-war.

There was plenty for us to get up to on the walk home - including a game of hedge hopping in the dark where we would jump over the garden hedges between the homes from Gray Gables to the cafe shortcut and back. This we would do when we were not tormenting Jim Alexander of course. All harmless fun and Jim Alexander was a really good sport.

U-Boat

Hacky and I were great pals growing up. The boys in our group all looked up to him as he was always the boss or the Chief Indian when we played cowboys and Indians. When we played soldiers, he would be the general or colonel.

On our first day at Lamlash Secondary School the local Lamlash boys tried to initiate the Brodick boys into our new school by attempting to dunk us under the water in the wash hand basins in the hallway. But they found their match with Hacky and I as we got the better of them and dunked them under the water instead. At playtime Hacky challenged any of them to a fisty-cuff fight and two of them stepped forward. He knocked the hell out of them both. This put paid to their initiation prank and thereafter they respected Hacky as a great fighter. What a guy!

Being a take charge type of guy, in part because he was the tallest in our group, Hacky became the captain of our ship in the following photograph. He even looked the part in his jacket, shirt with a tie, and wellie boots. Our ship for the day was one of the Brodick Bay swimmer life rafts that had broken loose and beached near the Douglas Hotel Burn, close to Brodick Pier. We claimed it for our ship and then decided to change it into a German U-boat with Hacky, thoroughly into his new captain role, barking out commands in a strong German accent.

L-R: Ken & Neil Page, John (Hacky) Hartley, myself, and Ross Cook N/D

Country Boys Go To Town!

Sandy Grieve's aunt that lived in Glasgow near the King's Theatre sent him a ticket to a Lonnie Donegan show as an early Christmas present. It just so happened that Hacky, Toby and I were also big fans of Lonnie Donegan. I remember how he sang '*My Old Man's a Dustman*' and '*Does Your Chewing Gum Lose It's Flavour (On the Bedpost Overnight).*' Sandy's aunt agreed to let us stay with her so we could all go to the show together. We thought that was a great idea but we only had a couple of months to save up enough money for this new venture.

Toby had a brain wave and suggested we could ask Johnny Stewart, at Spring Bank Farm, if we could shaw turnips for him to enable us to make enough money for our trip. The field that Johnny wanted us to work in was small and close to where we lived, allowing us to work every day we could to save our earnings for our first time off the island by ourselves. We were able to save a lot of money by Christmas; then came up with the idea of staying a second night so we could go to the carnival at Kelvin Hall.

The Lonnie Donegan concert was a huge success. But on our way to Kelvin Hall the next night, all was going well until Toby discovered his pocket had been picked and all his money stolen. The electric tram to the carnival had been packed solid, maybe that could have been where he lost his money, or perhaps when he had been standing in the long queue waiting to enter Kelvin Hall, as we had stood there mesmerized watching the sparks flying from the electric cables powering the tram cars as they passed by. We pooled together what money we had left and shared it evenly. This incident did not spoil our couple of days away on our own. We still had a great time at the Lonnie Donegan concert and the Kelvin Hall carnival where we spent most of the money we had left on chasing each other around in the bumper cars.

On our way back to Arran the next day the weather was very stormy at Ardrossan Harbour where giant waves crashed over the big sea wall. In those days the ferries sailed in all types of weather no matter what. We boarded the *Marchioness of Graham* at 6:00 p.m. and immediately made a beeline to the bow of the ship where we had great fun dodging the spray from the waves crashing onto the deck. A short time after leaving the harbour, we missed hearing the announcement for "All passengers are to stay inside as the outside doors would be locked for safety." Due to the darkness and the noise of the storm, no one saw us outside to warn us. By the time the ferry docked at Brodick, we were a bit wet and bedraggled to say the least.

58

To crown it all … I had purchased a 78 vinyl record of The Platters singing '*Only You*' for the Youth Club dances held at Curries Tearoom and had it concealed under my coat to keep it safe and dry. As I was going through the turnstile, where you had to pay thruppence to exit the pier, a loud crack could be heard and that was the end of the record.

Our trip away for two big nights of being out on our own was a great adventure despite a few hiccups and we all lived to tell the tale of "The country mice came to town."

Anyone for Tennis?

My first summer job was working with my uncle, David Drummond. He was the Brodick Hall keeper and was also in charge of maintaining the bowling green and the tennis courts. I was his assistant. First thing in the morning I had to sweep the red clay tennis courts and the white plastic lines.

The visitors were always chomping at the bit to get started arranging a tennis competition. Hacky and I were pretty good tennis players so we plucked up the courage to challenge the visitors. We did extremely well and even made it to the semifinals but could not take part in their final competition as it clashed with our commitment to play football for the Brodick team being held on the same Saturday. We could have won the tennis final. Who knows? Well, that's what we're saying!

Ally for Dally

Hacky, Toby, and I wanted to try our luck at burn trout fishing. As I was the only one that had a rod, we had to take turns using it. The decision was made to go fishing at a deep pool we called Dally's pool in the Cloy Burn. The pool was adjacent to George "Dally" Duncan's Vulcan Garage in Brodick.

While I was busy fishing, Hacky had been speaking to Dally and discovered he was planning to drive his lorry to the top of the String Road then cross over the hills on foot to the WW II plane crash site on Beinn Nuis to salvage scrap metal. He was looking for help to transport the scrap metal back to the lorry. As we were always looking for something to do, we volunteered to help him drag the aluminium scrap off of the mountain.

Dally arranged to borrow a horse and a big wooden sledge from Alister Davidson's small farm in Glen Rosa. Alister and his Clydesdale horse joined our team and we all hiked our way up to the crash site. Dally, Hacky, Toby, and I struggled like mad to free the fuselage embedded in the ground, then it was loaded onto the sledge and tied down tightly with ropes.

The smaller bits of aluminium scattered over a wide area were also gathered up, resulting in quite a large load for the poor horse to drag over the very rugged terrain. Hacky and I also had ropes attached to the sledge to enable us to assist the horse on the long, arduous trek back to the String Road. Toby followed along behind us retrieving the smaller aluminium pieces when they bounced off the back of the sledge.

Eventually, we made it to the String Road. The scrap was loaded onto Dally's lorry and driven to the dump at the pier for shipment to the mainland. This was yet another great adventure for us despite the hard work involved. We still had lots of fun and even came up with a jingle for our day's labour - "Ally for Dally!"

Army Cadets

After completing our education at Lamlash Secondary School, my pals and I joined the Army Cadets. Our cadet leader was Willie Allen, a joiner to trade. The cadet army hut was close to the Auchranie Hotel up Glen Cloy. The twelve members were made up of boys from Brodick, Corrie, and Lamlash villages. We participated in church parades, keep fit classes, and boxing matches. As cadets, we had the use of a small ex-army truck to perform army maneuvers out on the hills. We enjoyed rifle training and for safety reasons we would drive to the Southend of the island to practice target shooting into a steep hill where no hill walkers or hikers could be exposed to our training exercises. The rifle training that I received as an Army Cadet turned out to be beneficial to me later in life when I had the opportunity to become an assistant gamekeeper.

The cadets held an annual Christmas dance at their Brodick cadet hut. The girls that were invited from Whiting Bay and Shiskine were chauffeured to the cadet hut, though not exactly 'in style' as they had to huddle together in the back of the old army truck, driven by Tommy McLeod, in freezing cold weather. After the dance the girls had to climb back into the frigid army truck to be dropped off safely at their homes.

My record player provided the music for the dance but we soon discovered it had to stay at the far end of the hall as the record player needle would bounce off the track when we were dancing rock and roll too close to it. Despite the cold drive in the old army truck for the girls and the risk of sporadic stuttering from the record player, great fun was always had by all!

On the Road

When Hacky and I first obtained our driving license neither of us could afford a car, so we figured out a brilliant plan to solve our 'no car' predicament. We would go down to Lenox Garage at the pier when the Arran ferry came in with all the summer holiday makers onboard to offer our driving services to Jackie Lenox ... who was quite a creative businessman. He would regularly provide each of us with a car which enabled us to become his taxi drivers. Jackie didn't bother to pay us as we willingly drove just for the experience. To us this was great fun - not only were we getting driving experience, we were getting tips into the bargain!

We also sorted out our entertainment transportation dilemma on weekends. Hacky was an apprentice mechanic for Lenox Garage. Every Friday night in the summer he would ask Jackie if he could borrow a car to go to the dance in Lochranza. Consistently, Hacky managed to get a car and Jackie always told him "Use your own petrol." So, we would wait until the Lenox Garage was closed for the night, then walk down to where the buses were kept at the back of the building and syphon enough petrol from one of the buses to take us to the dance and back. In the late 1950s, you could get four gallons of petrol for £1. One good turn deserves another ... right!

Foosty's Boys in Blue

This is a story about Neil Kerr, a witty, cheery guy better known to us as Foosty. He was the manager of the Brodick football team and I must say that I think we had a really good team. The rivalry between Brodick and Lamlash was always pretty fierce. In my opinion, the two best players on Arran at that time were Bobby Cairns and Jim McGrory on the Brodick team.

I remember Ugo Pellegrini was the goalkeeper, then Archie McNicol took over followed by my pal Hacky. When we played against the Southend, big Davie Crosley was their goalkeeper and I believe he was also their manager. The Southend team was almost entirely made up of farmers and with the game being played in the middle of harvest time Davie ended up being a player short, so he had to negotiate with Foosty to borrow a substitute from the Brodick team until his full team arrived. Everyone just wanted to get the game started!

Don McIntyre, a nice quiet lad and a good football player, was selected to play on the Southend team. The game started and just ten minutes into the game Don scored a goal for the Southend. As you can imagine, there were a few choice words from the Brodick team.

I recall being in front of the goal about to shoot when this massive guy bundled me to the ground. It was one of the farmers known locally as '*the Twin*' who was old enough to be my faither and it was like hitting a brick wall! Not only was he a big man, but one of the hobnail boots he was wearing caught me on my right knee and I still have the scars to show for it.

At half time I asked Foosty, "Are we getting paid for this?" to which he replied, "Each player gets half an orange and Cappy (our team gofer) is going around the crowd with his hat collecting money to pay for a Ribbick's bus for the next away game. What more do you want?"

Another game we had against Shiskine with Foosty in charge was at the Bainacoole Stadium. When we arrived, Foosty suggested we clear the coos out of the park and lift the coo pats, the dry ones that is. This was early spring with fresh new grass and with cows eating new grass … you can imagine the mess we ended up in. Worst of all Ribbick's Garage, our team sponsor, had just provided us with new team jerseys that wound up looking as bad as our white shorts from being splattered with a mixture of green grass, blood, spit, etc. Talk about health and safety - there should have been a nurse on standby to give out tetanus injections.

When the game was over, we had planned to go to the bus to get changed but the bus had mysteriously disappeared. It was found down at the Hamilton Arms, a friendly pub, a couple of hundred yards away. When we asked the slightly tipsy driver why he had left the football park with some of the supporters he claimed, "The midges were really bad." Good one! No midges were out on that cool windy evening and we knew it was all about any excuse will do to get to the pub. Luckily for us Hacky had recently attained his PSV license and drove the bus back to Brodick.

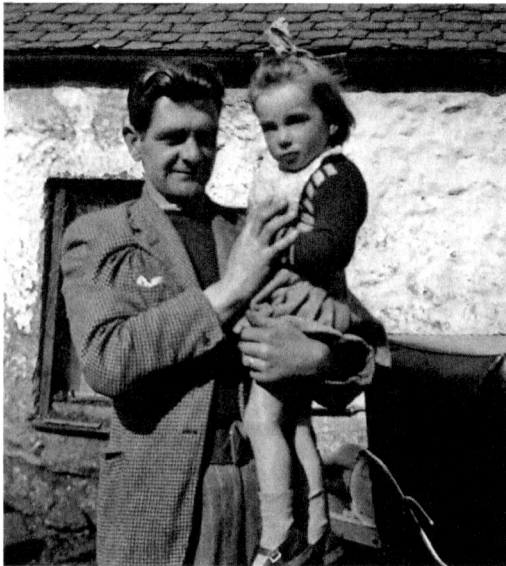

Neil (Foosty) Kerr with his niece, Sheena McCrae N/D

Chapter 3 - WEDDING DAY

Brodick Church

Rosemary and I were married in Brodick Church. We had known each other throughout our schooldays. Sadly, Rosemary passed away in September 2020 after 57 years of marriage.

As I was looking through old photographs, I found a Certificate of Excellence she had achieved for her handwriting in a competition representing Brodick Primary School, where she had been the winner out of many other participants. I also discovered her DUX Certificate of Excellence from Brodick school. Something else she had kept quiet about. If it had been me, I would have had it in all the newspapers!

I was nearly DUX at the school. We were in the same class and sat across from each other. On test days, which was every Friday, I would copy her exam paper and always received high marks. This was working out great for me until one Friday we fell out about something and as we sat down to take the test, Rosemary covered her test paper with her elbow. So that was me snookered!

Mr. Brodie was a teacher and also the headmaster of Brodick Primary school. He was a short, portly, no-nonsense type of person that always wore a brown suit, dress shirt and tie. As he was marking our test papers that day, he paused several times to look directly at me then back at the papers on his desk. He then announced that Rosemary had the highest marks as usual. When the class was dismissed for the day, Mr. Brodie called me over to his desk and inquired, "Would I be correct in saying that you have been copying Rosemary's test papers all along." To which I cautiously replied, "Yes, Sir." He proceeded to lecture me about cheating, ending the conversation by telling me, "You'll never get anywhere in this world." I left the classroom feeling disappointed at being caught cheating. So, if you take my advice, never fall out with the person you copy from. I'm not stupid - I married her!

Looks like I scrubbed up pretty well for our wedding day considering what was done to me the night before! After we had returned from the wedding rehearsal, a gang of women chased me into my soon to be in-laws house. They caught me as I attempted to make a mad dash into the bathroom to shut and lock the door. They stuck me down on the toilet and had Elinor Hartley (Hacky's sister) sit on top of me while the others removed my shoes and socks then proceeded to cover my feet with black shoe polish. Not only were my feet blackened, I ended up covered in shoe polish right up to my knees!

To top things off the girls took immense pleasure in applying rouge, lipstick, and eye shadow to my face. What a sight I must have made that night, but at least there is no sign of the black shoe polish or makeup in the wedding photo. Foot blackening and face painting used to be a common Arran tradition the night before a couple's wedding day.

Following the ceremony at Brodick Church our reception was held in the Douglas Hotel a short distance from Brodick Pier. When it was time for us to leave the reception to catch the Arran ferry and head off on our honeymoon, my pals sat us on the old iron luggage barrow to wheel us down to the pier. The same old luggage barrow that was used in the television comedy series Para Handy about a crew on a puffer coal boat called the *Vital Spark*. A few of the episodes in the series had been filmed in Brodick.

In the photograph of me standing at the bottom of the ferry gangway I was saying, "Right, what have you done with my wife, has she done a bunk?" There are a few 'well kent' faces in the background. I don't know what Don McIntye is pointing at in the photo but what I do know is that he was the bugger that scored the goal for the Southend football team when he was on loan from the Brodick team.

We went off on our honeymoon to Aberdeen and on our return moved into the main house at number 3 Douglas Row that Lady Jean had generously offered to me rent free as part of my wages.

L-R: Don McIntyre, Fanny McKinnie, my dad, Mimi Hogg, Mrs. Selkirk, myself, Bertie Sillars, Morag McIntyre, Alister Douglas, & Mrs. Cook - 6 November 1963

Shark!

Shortly after Rosemary and I were married, we decided to hire a rowing boat to go out fishing in Brodick Bay. I think it was one shilling for an hour of fishing. The bay was very busy that night with locals and visitors fishing. The Arran ferry was docked at the pier and some of the visitors were unaware that the ferry would make a wide sweep around the bay blasting its horn as it left the pier to warn the boats to scatter out of the way as the ferry headed out to sea to make its way across to Ardrossan Harbour.

That same evening a number of basking sharks were cruising around in the calm bay water as my wife and I were quietly fishing. One of the basking sharks came way too close to our boat and Rosemary started screaming, "Take me back to the shore!" I kept trying to calm her down by assuring her that basking sharks were harmless but she was having none of it, so we immediately pulled up our fishing lines. Rosemary was in such a panic to get away from the shark circling around our boat that I did not stop to pull up the anchor, and ended up rowing the boat all the way back to the shore dragging the anchor. No wonder I was knackered when we finally did make it to the shore!

The McKinnie Picnic

The annual McKinnie picnic held at Glen Rosa was something we looked forward to as it was always a great day full of fun. Just past Davidson's Farm the Rosaburn has a very large natural bathing pool, not too deep, and safe for the kids to go swimming. There is also a flat grass area ideal for playing games. Scotland against England teams would be picked for a game of rounders. Even the campers in the nearby area would ask to join in.

This gathering of family and friends must have amounted to over 20 attendees. John Corbet, Sr., a McKinnie relative, was the head cook for the huge barbecue. The men would guddle for fish in the burn and what they caught would end up on the barbecue.

In the evening the men would build a big bonfire and as the fire was burning down, everyone would gather around to roast tatties on long sticks cut from trees in the area. The tatties would end up black on the outside and were eaten in spite of being a bit raw on the inside. Still, no one was poisoned.

Fun at the McKinnie Picnic N/D

Chapter 4 - HOME FARM

The Bull Pole

At the time I joined the Home Farm workforce in 1957, Gerald Murray was the Farm Manager and Jimmy Mitchell was the first tractor man. Later on I became a tractor man as did my good friend Bob McIntyre (Bob was quite a character as you will soon find out). Bob Buchanan was employed as the dairyman. He was a wee heavy-set man that liked to laugh at his own jokes and had teeth that looked like a row of condemned hooses. Miss Jean Gordon was the dairymaid and she had an unusual job description as you will soon read about in this story. Neil Shaw was the piggery man and Sandy Kerr was the shepherd. A few years later on Bob Todd became the dairyman and Ross Cook was his assistant.

A couple of years after I had started working at the farm, Lady Jean decided to phase out her herd of Red Pole cows and replace them with an Ayrshire breed because the Ayrshire cows were better milk producers. Their milk had a much higher butter fat content and they were less costly to feed. Scottish farmers also phasing out their Red Pole herds for the same reasons as Lady Jean, therefore, they did not need to keep their bulls as the Red Pole breed was being made redundant.

Lady Jean received word that she had the only Red Pole bull left for breeding in Scotland making her bull the sperm donor for all the remaining Red Pole cows throughout Scotland. The bull was kept in a pen stronghold at the back of the farm and what a huge, muscular, intimidating beast he was. As his legs were shorter than the Red Pole cows, it did create a bit of a problem when a cow came in season at breeding time. To compensate for the height difference the cow was reversed into a specially built ramp to enable the bull to reach her for mating.

Miss Jean Gordon became the self-appointed chief sperm catcher. She was a small, stooped, elderly spinster. Her job was to skillfully deviate from the normal mating ritual by capturing the sperm into a bottle instead of the cow … to the great amusement of the men watching. All the farm workers were required to attend this event for safety reasons to ensure the bull did not fall off his perch while he thought he was servicing the cow. On a couple of occasions the bull did lose his balance and Miss Gordon had to be pulled out of harms way. Well, you did request more stories … so this is nature getting a helping hand!

(Can you imagine Miss Gordon going down to the Job Centre nowadays looking for employment and being asked by a girl behind the desk, "What was your last job?" Her response to Miss Gordon would be, "There's not many jobs like that available now!")

Back to the story ... Bob Buchanan went off to fetch the bull. To control the bull he had a pole with a clip on the end that attached to the bull's nose ring as a means of restraining him if necessary. When the end of the pole was jammed into the ground, it would shove the bull's head up into the air to stop him. That must have hurt him! This time the bull became a bit frisky as he knew where he was going and all of a sudden he broke loose and went charging round the back of the cow shed.

That day Lady Jean had been baking for a local whist drive she was going to and had run out of milk so she sent Shring, the wee man from India that worked in the kitchen, to the farm for milk. Just as Shring turned the corner of the cow shed he came face to face with the charging bull and got the absolute fright of his life. Poor Shring, he had never seen a bull this massive in his life. He tossed the tin milk can in the air and darted into the big silo pit beside him and slammed the door shut.

Once we had the bull under control we had to persuade Shring to come out of the silo and, yes, the bull had run over the milk can and it was bashed in. Raymond McClain, the odd job man at the farm, offered to escort Shring back to Strabane House as the wee man was so traumatized from the shock he just had. In fact, Shring was shaking so badly he had trouble trying to fit the lid back onto the bashed up milk can. I don't know what kind of story they gave to Lady Jean. I am just glad I was not there!

The bull pole turned out to be quite a versatile tool around the farm that Robert Middleton, a very quiet man with a witty sense of humour, and I found to be useful for catching pheasants in the fir trees behind the farm.

We would take a handful of corn that had been soaked in whisky and leave it out for the pheasants to eat before they went to roost in the trees at night. When it was dark, we would shine a bright torch light up into the trees to dazzle the now tipsy pheasants roosting, hence enabling us to easily slip the bull pole clip over their heads and pull them down from the trees. Bingo! That was the next day's dinner.

The Home Farm always had plenty of pheasants around as Lady Jean bred them for game shooting. And we were silent killers!

L-R: Bob McIntye, Neil Shaw, Gordon Shaw, & myself. Not much farm work today. Too busy posing for photographs circa 1958

L-R Myself, Neil Shaw, Sandy Kerr, Bob Todd's twins and Bob McIntyre N/D

I came in second last in this late 1950s ploughing competition, but I did win the sprinting race across the ploughed up field in my donkey jacket and wellie boots.

Tattie Howkin'

This wee story is about my friend and workmate, Bob McIntyre. He was a great guy to work with as he was always up to mischief, anything for a good laugh, and we did have many good laughs. Bob never wore his false teeth (top or bottom), smoked 'Thick Black' tobacco in his long curly pipe and when Bob was amused, he would toss his head back with mouth wide open and let loose with boisterous laughter. In the winter he usually had a dreep running from his nose that would be attached to his long pipe or he had a dribble sliding down his chin. His hair was always a bit tousled. His nickname was Touser - I wonder why?

Bob and I were working with a large squad of tattie howkers in a huge field at the Home Farm in early October. In other words we were harvesting a potato crop with pickers made up of travelling people and school children. The schools would release kids for one or two weeks when they volunteered to assist farmers bring in their potato crops. There was always plenty of volunteers and they were guaranteed a good feed at lunchtime with sandwiches and a tin cup full of strong, sweetened tea. Sometimes the pickers were fortunate enough to be provided with a hearty sit-down meal at a farmhouse.

The pickers had the job of picking up the potatoes by hand and placing them into a basket. The baskets were emptied into burlap sacks and then the sacks were loaded onto a trailer for Bob to drive them back to the farm storage shed. When the shed at the farm was full of tatties, Bob would start a tattie pit at the edge of the field and cover them with rushes and soil to keep them fresh until they were needed.

When we broke for lunch, we all gathered together and sat behind the big beech hedge in the field to keep out of the cold wind. As this was early October, the leaves on the hedge were a bit sparse. During lunch one of the picker women slipped behind the hedge as nature was calling and Bob's eagle eyes spotted her. As she got down to business facing away from us Bob pushed his shovel under the hedge, under her and caught the thing, then he pulled the shovel back through the hedge. When she was finished, she turned around and 'it' was gone. Next she checked her wellie boots in case it had dropped inside. When she returned to our group she, had a perplexed look on her face until she heard Bob and I laughing.

My good friend Bob (Touser) McIntyre (You can see the devilment in his face.) circa 1958

Highland Fling

This was a day when the laughs were on Bob McIntyre for a change. As we were moving the old thrashing mill from the barn to the stack yard, mice were darting about in all directions as the equipment was being relocated. One ran up the leg of Bob's trousers and I don't know what dance he was doing but it looked a lot like the Highland Fling.

On another occasion, he trapped a big rat in the corner of the barn and was about to stab it with a pitchfork when the damn thing ran right up the shaft of the pitchfork, over his shoulder, and away. The following day he set a trap hoping to catch the rat. The next morning he checked the trap and only a snared leg was left in it. The rat must have chewed through its leg to escape. The joys of working on a farm! Well, someone had to do it.

Catacol Glen

In the late 1950s I was on the estate workers team tasked with building a deer fence around whitebeam trees that had been discovered in Catacol Glen to protect them from being damaged by the deer. Lady Jean explained that the reason the whitebeams were being fenced in was because they were a rare type of rowan tree that needed to be safeguarded.

The seeds must have been dropped in Catacol Glen by migrating birds. The estate had to hire a helicopter to deliver all the heavy fencing material to the remote area in the glen and it took weeks for the estate workers to complete the fencing project

The Arran whitebeam trees are among the most endangered tree species in the world.

This Whitebeam L Sorbus Arranensis is on display behind Brodick Castle
2 July 2021

88

The Old Cottage

Another interesting day I recall was when I was selected to accompany Duncan Langlands to the sawmill to load logs. Duncan was a wee wiry man, a heavy smoker and always very witty. We loaded the estate lorry up with as big a load of firewood as possible for delivery to an elderly couple in their eighties that lived in an old stone cottage near Imnacher Farm in Machrie. As we approached the cottage, Duncan noticed that the thatched roof had been replaced with a tin roof. The old man explained to us that he had set fire to the inside of the chimney to burn off thick soot. Unfortunately, the fire somehow leaked through the chimney breast and ignited the thatched roof. He admitted to us he should have had the chimney sweep do the job for him.

Life in the cottage would seem very primitive to us nowadays. There was an old mangle for wringing water out of the 'washing' (laundry) and a hand washboard was propped against the wall outside the front door. The toilet was outside at the back of the house.

After we had offloaded the firewood the lady of the house invited us in for a cup of tea. The little cottage, like many of those in that era, had very small windows making it quite dark inside. A big black kettle hung from a chain over the fireplace. The mantlepiece was decorated with a couple of big toby jugs. She handed us each an old tin cup filled with tea and we had to use our teeth to strain off the floating tea leaves. The tea was black as night and didn't taste very good as she had just added a handful of tea leaves and more hot water to the tea pot that was already sitting beside the stove. The tea pot must have been stewing away since breakfast time. The handle on the tin cup was quite hot so I sat it down on the floor and discovered it was an earth floor. The legs of the chair I was sitting on had actually sunk into the ground. The old lady offered me a grated carrot sandwich and I must say, this was a first for me. When I was a kid, I used to get a sandwich made with HP sauce, tomato sauce or a butter and sugar one ... definitely no carrot ones.

She offered Duncan the same but he refused saying he was "going out for a smoke." When Duncan finished his cigarette, he came back into the house for a wee blether. We enjoyed our blether with the old couple as they were remarkably interesting. They told us that neither of them had ever been off the island since they were born and saw no reason to ever have to leave as the island provided them with all that they needed. And spoke about how it was the norm when they were getting married for villagers in the area to come and help them start building a cottage that was wind and water tight, then they completed the rest themselves.

The bedroom door was open and from where I was sitting, I could see an ancient chanty pot tucked under their bed. No TV! They did have an old wireless set sitting on a small table in the corner of the kitchen that was crackling away.

There was no need for me to worry about my carrot sandwich crumbs getting on the floor as the hens were doing an excellent job of cleaning up any that dropped. The hens were circling all around my chair like they were part of the family.

The old couple's cottage - 2 July 2021

91

Tree Thinning

One nice summer day Harry Smye, Duncan Langlands, Kenny Bain, Bob McIntyre, Bob Cameron, and I were working on thinning out trees in the Glen Rosa forest just before the gate at the deer fence. We had stopped for our morning tea break and were all sitting on a steep embankment chatting away as a bunch of hikers passed by heading for the hills. One of the girls was caught short (she probably had a curry the night before), she jumped over the stone dyke then crouched down behind a tree to take care of business.

Bob McIntyre, full of mischief as usual, bet each of us one shilling that she would not wipe her bum; then in his robust loud voice shouted out, "What do you think you are doing?" She was up with her pants, leapt over the stone dyke and running to catch up with the rest of her group, still trying to adjust herself. She must have had an extremely uncomfortable day out on the hills. We spent the rest of the day laughing at her misfortune. Bob was fair pleased with himself about winning his crafty little bet and we had to pay up.

Fire!

Lady Jean had tasked six estate workers (Harry Smye, Duncan Langlands, Kenny Bain, Bob McIntyre, Bob Cameron, and me) with burning heather at the top of Glen Cloy as she wanted new heather to grow there in order to attract grouse to return to that hillside. Grouse prefer to feed on the seeds of new heather. The hill at the top of the glen is called the Windmill and it was well named.

In August through September the hills become striking patches of blooming purple heather all over the island … an amazing sight to see. White heather is mainly found in home gardens. Some people consider a sprig of white heather to be a good luck charm. In autumn the bracken on the hills changes from green to orange/brown patches.

When we started the fire, it began burning as fast as we could walk. Then the wind gusts changed to an easterly direction making the fire blow right up the glen fanning the flames. The heather came up to our knees because it had not been burned for years. Consequently, the fire was soon well out of our control. We all started to panic! If the fire went over the top of the hill, it could result in miles of forest on the other side being in jeopardy.

It took us hours to beat the flames back. By the time we had extinguished the fire it was past midnight and we were all completely exhausted, hungry, and reeking of smoke. Harry Smye, a boy scout leader, took charge of the situation as it was now pitch dark and you could not even see the person standing right next to you. He instructed us to link our brooms together and walk in a line listening for the sound of the water in the Cloy Burn as that would help guide us back to the main road. Our group must have looked like recruits from the television comedy show Dad's Army as we stumbled around in the heather. Just as well nobody could have seen us, invisible as we were, in the pitch darkness.

Luckily our fire in Glen Cloy did not burn for too long. But most people from Brodick may remember the fire up in Glen Shant, the hill on the right hand side when walking up Glen Rosa. Not sure how this fire started, but it smoldered among the rocks for about two years. It must have been caused from the heather roots embedded under the cliff face that kept it smoldering at night for so long. You could see the fire glowing from the village, especially when the east wind blew.

The Entrepreneur

Lady Jean tried her hand at many different business ventures. One of her greatest successes was her pointer show dogs. She was very fond of all her pointers and springer spaniels, especially her two champion pointers that won many trophies in dog trials all over Britain. I had the pleasure of working with them during grouse shooting season.

The Home Farm had a contract to supply the island Southend Creamery with milk. Any excess milk was used for her new venture of dispensing different flavoured milk into the vending machines that had been installed at the Brodick Pier and the Brodick Putting Green. Robert Middleton and I were given the job of filling the machines up twice daily when milk was available. This was not a great success.

She also tried a marmalade factory and that did not do well either. At one point I said to her, "Milady, I think you are a bit of a jinx!" She gave me a hearty, good natured slap on the shoulder and walked away laughing.

Another of Lady Jean's endeavours was market gardening at the farm which did do a bit better. One field was used to plant garden peas and carrots while another field had lettuce, cabbage, and green beans. A third field was planted with raspberries and strawberries. The fields were located on the right-hand side of the shortcut footpath from the Rosaburn Smiddy to the main Corrie Road. (The old Smiddy is now one of many exhibits at The Isle of Arran Heritage Museum in Brodick.)

Unfortunately, the fields were full of all the foodstuff that pigeons liked to eat. When she realised that the pigeons were having a great time sampling whatever they felt like in the fields, she decided to buy an automatic gun that would bang every ten minutes to frighten the pigeons away. The problem was that it scared the wits out of everything and everybody around Brodick. This gun was as loud as the one o'clock gun fired at Edinburgh Castle!

Lady Jean met Howard and me at a field to provide us with the instruction book on how to set up the automatic gun. The instructions were extremely complicated. Water dripped into a chamber of chemicals that caused an explosion, and what an explosion. The loud 'BANG' could even be heard miles away at Brodick Pier. At first we had it going off every two minutes, then every 15 minutes. The timer was really difficult to set.

A group of day trippers on hired bikes came cycling along the shortcut and just as they were passing by us the damn thing went off. You should have seen them crashing into one another from the shock they got. They were a bit wobbly on the bikes anyway. While we were still studying the instructions, the damn thing went off again. A passing car on the main Corrie Road came to a stop for the driver to get out to check his tyres - thinking he had a blow out. Howard and I were giggling behind the hedge. Eventually, we managed to set it to go off properly. Lady Jean appeared to tell us that she had been listening for the bangs at Strabane House and was pleased we now had it set to go off every ten minutes and left satisfied with her new action plan.

As we were about to leave the field, the police arrived because there had been a number of complaints reported regarding the repetitive loud banging noises in the area. Howard advised them that Lady Jean was at home and it would be better for them to speak to her. They were about to get into their car to leave, when the damn thing went off again. I believe they had a very good case.

Lady Jean decided that as I lived close by, I should come over and shut the gun off in the evening and start it up again at 8:00 a.m. The only thing wrong with that was the pigeons started eating at 6:00 a.m. and were fully fed and leaving by 8:00 a.m. This was a short-lived venture ... the pigeons won!

When I was going through my house looking for family photographs for this book, I happened to come across the two autobiographical books Lady Jean had written. She wrote about growing up in two castles, participating in royal events, her extensive travels, getting married, and candidly disclosed her family's successes and tragedies.

In 1982 Lady Jean presented my Aunt Elsie with a signed copy of her first published book, *Castles in the Air* with a personal note inside. Her second book, *Feet on the Ground - from Castles to Catastrophe*, was published in 2001. They are extremely interesting books to read. So in my opinion, she was also a successful author.

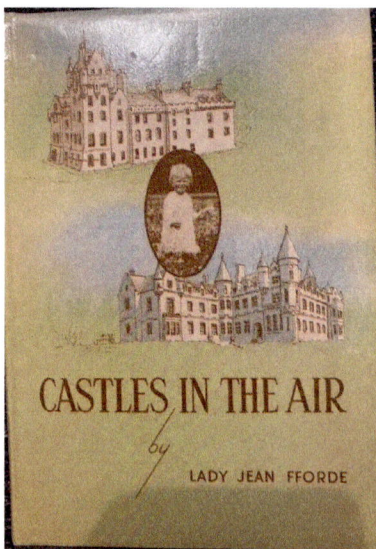

Castles in the Air 1982

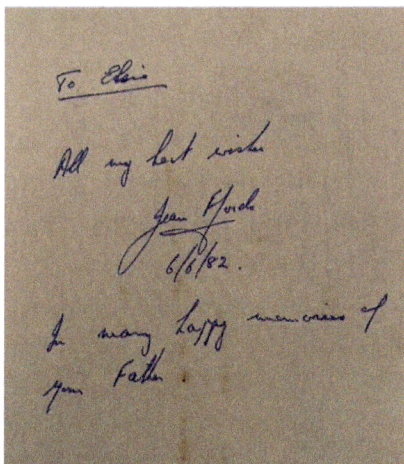

Lady Jean's message: "To Elsie, All my best wishes - Jean Fforde 6/6/82 - In many happy memories of your Father."

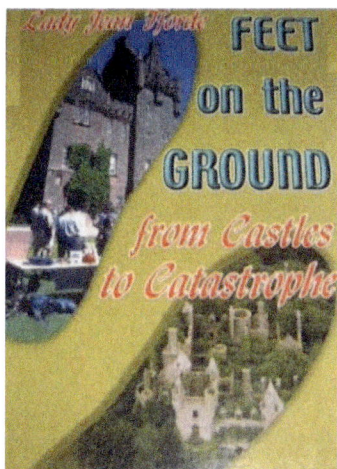

Feet on the Ground - from Castles to Catastrophe 2001

Chance

Bob McIntyre had a lovely big black and white collie dog named Chance. He was Bob's faithful companion. Bob enjoyed his trips to the pub where Chance would settle quietly under Bob's table. Everyone made a great fuss over the dog. When Bob was ready to make his way home, Chance followed along right at his heels.

One very cold, frosty winters night on my way home from playing badminton in Brodick Hall, I came across Bob lying on the side of the road leading up to Douglas Row. His clothes were actually frozen to the ground and Chance was snuggled beside him like he was trying to keep him warm. I quickly stopped in at my house to tell Rosemary about the situation then walked on to Bob's house to make sure there was a good fire stoked up to help thaw him out when I did get him back to the house.

Chance was fine with me helping his master into the house but would not let me out the door to go home. Obviously, he wanted me to stay there. Luckily for me I had stopped at my house to let my wife know I was seeing Bob home because after a while of wondering what was keeping me, she came looking for me and was able to help me escape.

(This is a similar story to the previous one. A drunk man staggering home from the pub comes across a cat lying at the side of the road. As he went over to say hello to it, he was violently sick all over the poor animal. The man thought to himself, "I don't remember eating all that!")

Another wee story about Chance: At shearing time Bob and I would give the shepherd a hand to pen the sheep at the farm. Chance had never been trained to herd sheep. He was strictly Bob's loyal companion. When Sandy Kerr, the shy easygoing shepherd, directed his two collie dogs to round up the sheep that were scattered all over the field, Chance automatically followed the two collies and did a fantastic job of taking part in herding the sheep into the pens. He was a natural!

Bob was so proud of Chance and could not believe how his untrained dog had taken to the task at hand. Even Chance seemed to be pleased with himself as he lay at Bob's feet being praised for "What a grand job he had done with the sheep!"

Catch of the Day

One summer fifteen boats participated in a fishing contest in Brodick Bay. I was in Lady Jean's boat with her son, Charles, Peter Hume and Howard Walker. John Basford, the head gardener and an avid fisherman, had told me that the best place for us to fish was off Strabane House by lining up the house chimney pots with the top of the String Road as a guide. He was spot on! We won first prize for the best catch of the day.

Between the 15 boats there must have been close to a ton of fish caught. After the weigh-in was judged, a load of fish was delivered to Lamlash Hospital, a load was packed up for shipment to Raven's Park Hospital in Irvine and the rest was shared among the locals, including visitors staying at the island's self-catering accommodations. A really successful day of fishing was enjoyed by all the participants.

Lady Jean's Strabane House - 14 June 2022

From Arran to Dubai

Another important job I had at the Arran Estate was assisting the head forester, Alistair Douglas. He was a tall, slim, outgoing man that liked hill climbing and bird watching. Alistair was responsible for carefully choosing which of the huge sycamore trees on the castle grounds were to be cut down by Duncan Mullholand, the hired contractor. It was my job to carry a pot of paint to mark a cross on the trees that were to be felled for a monumental project.

The selected trees were transported to the Cladach sawmill to be cut into huge wooden planks that were shipped to the mainland where they were to be installed as flooring in the ballroom of the RMS *Queen Elizabeth 2* ocean liner that was being built in the 1960s at the John Brown Shipyard on the River Clyde. In 1968 the RMS *Queen Elizabeth 2* performed speed trials off the Isle of Arran's coast.

The woodgrain pattern of the sycamore trees polished up into a first-class shiny finished surface fit for a Queen. So, if you ever have the chance to travel to Dubai, where the RMS *Queen Elizabeth 2* is currently anchored and has been renovated into a floating hotel, you can tell everyone on the ship that the special wooden floor in the ballroom came from a wee Scottish Island called the Isle of Arran.

Why The Long Face?

Another funny story about the Home Farm! On a very warm night as I was on my way to bed, I opened the upstairs bedroom window wide and could hear someone singing away in the distance. Sure enough it turned out to be Bob McIntyre coming home from the pub singing his favourite song "Isle of Arran, Isle of Beauty." He only knew the first verse so it was definitely Bob. He lived at number 8 Douglas Row. There was someone with him and I recognised the voice of Tommy Stewart, a heavy-set man with a loud laugh just like Bob's laugh. He was the horseman who worked the two big Clydesdales that dragged the timber off the hills down to the sawmill. Tommy stayed at the foot of Douglas Row in the bothy. I called out to Bob as he was passing that I would pick him up in the morning, he responded, "Aye Right!" and continued singing the Isle of Arran song.

(Another wee side step: Bob told me about his pal, Tommy, having a glass eye and when they were sitting in the pub having a pint, if Tommy had to go to the toilet he would take out his glass eye, place it next to his drink and say, "Keep an eye on that." Still makes me laugh thinking about it to this day.)

Lady Jean had given me the job of taking six sheep to the Lamlash Cattle Show that was to be held at the Lamlash football field. I also had to pick up a borrowed horse box from a neighbouring farmer, Alistair Davidson. On the morning of the show Bob was to go with me to help pick up the sheep.

I went to work on the morning of the show, picked up the tractor, the horse box, and then the sheep. No Bob anywhere! There was still no sign of Bob when I drove back to Douglas Row hoping to find him at his house. Finally, I found him at Tommy's house having breakfast and my friend was wondering what all the fuss was about, so I had to remind him about the cattle show.

Driving through Brodick on our way to the event, Bob was perched on the tractor mud guard shouting out to everyone, especially the women. On our way down into Lamlash the police stopped us. The constable informed me that the trailer's rear brake lights were not working. I explained that neither the tractor nor trailer had lights. He then wanted to know who the tractor belonged to. I replied, "Lady Jean and you will have to speak to her."

After we arrived at the show grounds and had everything set up, Bob announced he was just going to the beer tent as he was a bit dry. While there he ran into two of Lady Jean's guests. He had met them before at the farm. They were also in the tent for their daily tipple. Bob invited them over to have a look at Lady Jean's pen of sheep. One was Lady Margaret and the other was Lady Silvia. They were the Scottish aristocrats that had been out shooting grouse the year before. I, too, knew them both.

By now you must be aware that Bob is always out for a good laugh and boy did he get one this time. There was a pen with cows next to where we were standing beside the sheep pen and Lady Margaret said to Bob, "Why do cows have such long, mournful faces?" Quick as a flash he answered in his booming voice, "Milady, if you had your tits pulled twice a day and nooky once a year, you would have a long, mournful face too." This caused an uproar of laughter from the crowd that had gathered in the area. The two ladies walked away arm in arm snickering to themselves. Well, I told you Bob had a loud voice and enjoyed a good laugh!

Chapter 5 - DEER STALKING

Kitted Out in Khaki

Howard Walker was the head gamekeeper and I was his assistant. We had the job of taking Lady Jean's guests deer stalking. The far north of the island was Howard's beat and if there were two guests I would take one of them and head up to Glen Rosa, my favourite glen, or over the String Road to Shiskine.

Howard was always sharply dressed in his khaki outfit with his deer stalker hat and he enjoyed smoking his curly pipe. So for my first shoot with Lady Jean, she offered to rig me out with a khaki uniform and handed me one of her ex-Army gear outfits that was two sizes too big for me. Lady Jean was dressed in her old Land Army uniform including her pillbox hat. We were both wearing nicky-tams to raise our trousers above the mud level and to keep the heather seeds from going into our boots.

(During the Second World War Lady Jean was one of thousands of women who became a codebreaker at the Government Code and Cypher School at Bletchley Park in Buckinghamshire, England. Through their successful code breaking work, the women were credited with cracking the German codes and received recognition for helping to save lives and ending the war by at least two years.)

Off we went laughing at each other dressed in our khaki outfits looking like characters that had escaped from 'Dad's Army.' We headed for Glen Rosa, then up to Glen Shant where I spotted the old stag through the binoculars that she wanted to shoot. It must have taken us a good hour to crawl up the deep ditch to get to within shooting distance of the stag.

Lady Jean was ahead of me and her method of crawling was not good for stalking deer, partly because she was six feet tall. Trying to crawl without your knees touching the ground can make your backside stick up considerably. That's when I forgot myself for a moment and said, "Milady, will you please keep your backside down a bit." She responded with a snigger. When she did manage to master crawling better, guess what ... she stopped suddenly and I bumped into her backside head first. That ended the shoot because of all the laughter. As I looked up over the top of the ditch, the stag was disappearing over the horizon.

Coming down off the hill we passed some hikers who gave us funny looks. We must have been quite a sight to see as we were covered in black peat mud from crawling in the ditch and a bit bedraggled looking as we headed back to Strabane House. The hikers would never have guessed that she owned this part of the island.

109

Lady Jean employed Shring to help out in the kitchen and Mrs. Hume, a local, who did all the cooking when Milady had guests. As Shring ran out to greet us wanting to see a stag up close for the first time and there wasn't one, Lady Jean introduced me to him. He turned to me and said, "My name Shring. If you want me, just Shring! Ha, Ha, Ha!" I thought that was quite a good end to a really fun day.

When I picked up Mrs Hume to drive her to Strabane House the next morning, she mentioned that as she was serving the guests in the dining room last evening, there was great laughter as Lady Jean was telling them about our crawling escapade and what I had said to her about her backside sticking up. Mrs Hume told me that if I had said that to the Duchess, I would have been clapped in irons or locked up in the castle dungeon. Lucky for me Lady Jean had such an exceptional sense of humour.

The Haflinger

Around 1961, Lady Jean made arrangements with the Nature Conservancy in Edinburgh to recruit four students to come to Arran to work for her. The Nature Conservancy was in charge of calculating the number of male and female deer to be culled on the island each year.

The students were assigned to start counting deer in March as that was the best time of year to count them. The hinds would be grouped together in herds before calving in May/June and all the stags gathered in big herds making it easy for them to be counted as well. Their next task was working in the castle gardens until September when it was time for the deer culling to start. Her guests shot over one hundred stags that year. Lady Jean, Charles, Howard and I shot the rest to achieve the designated quotas. The students were also hired to drag the culled deer bodies off the hills.

That was the year Lady Jean had purchased a small Steyr-Puch Haflinger all-terrain vehicle that could go anywhere on the island with the added feature that all four wheels could be locked into four-wheel drive. She instructed Howard and me to take the four students out to introduce them to the job and allowed Howard to drive her precious Haflinger vehicle. Howard and I each shot a big stag above Stewart Lambie's farm in Glen Shurig.

111

As we were driving down the steep hill with the two big stags and two of the students in the back of the Haflinger, near the bottom of the hill, Howard had to turn a hard left to avoid a deep ditch. Just as he made the turn to cross over the hill the front wheel hit a big rock that was covered in moss. Over we went, flipping two or three times. When we finally came to a stop, Howard jumped out of the Haflinger and was hopping about like a mad man. He had been smoking his curly pipe and the hot tobacco ash had dropped inside his shirt.

Our greater concern was the apparent condition of the two students in the back of the Haflinger, as they were tangled up together with the two dead stags and they were covered in blood. They looked terrible until we discovered it was the stags' blood not the students' blood. The blood on them had spilled out of the gutted deer carcasses and the stags' antlers had ripped holes in the Haflinger's canvas cover. When the other two students that were walking down the hill caught up with the scene, they were shocked to see the state their colleagues were in ... then relieved that their pals were not injured.

On the way back to the kennels Howard asked, "Are you going to tell her?" I replied, " You can tell her it was you that was driving." Howard then said, "But you know her better than me." I replied, "That's why I'm not telling her!"

Anyway, we off-loaded the stags at the kennels, then Howard and I went to see Peter Hume, the estate mechanic, to see if he could repair the Haflinger canvas roof. Peter managed to patch the roof using a needle and thread to sew the torn canvas back together then Howard and I washed the vehicle inside and out to make it somewhat presentable. When we returned to Strabane House, we met with Lady Jean and sheepishly confessed to what had happened. She took the news very well, so we rushed away to pick up the two students we had left behind at Glen Shurig. Thank goodness she was in a good mood that day.

Locked Horns

Geologists would flock to Arran to study the unusual rocks and stones found on the island. Apparently they are unique to Arran and not found anywhere else in Scotland. Some of the points of interest the geologists had the opportunity to explore included the historic Machrie Moor stone circle, the King's Cave near Drumadoon Farm with its carvings dating back thousands of years, arrow heads and pottery artifacts that have been discovered on the island for years. So much ancient history on such a small island!

I remember seeing the geologists chapping away at the rocks around the Brodick Primary school grounds when we had playtime at school years ago. But having geologists swarming all over the hills can make things a bit problematic for any hunting season.

Around 1962 a group of visiting geologists, returning from a day out on the hills, left word at the kennels that two stags had locked antlers and had remained that way all day. The following day Lady Jean heard about the stags with locked antlers and quickly rearranged our day. Howard was to take one of her guests to North Sannox and I would be taking her out to see if anything could be done to free the two stags. We made our way to Glen Shant with two of the hired students and soon found the exhausted stags … bleeding and in poor condition. Lady

Jean and I agreed they must be shot. After she shot the stags we discovered that there was no way that they could ever have been separated.

Once I had gutted them and cut their antlers free with a hacksaw from the Haflinger toolbox, Lady Jean and I went off to make a day of shooting out on the hills. The students were left to drag the deer off of the hill, load them into the Haflinger, drive to the kennel storage area to unload, and return to Glen Shant to pick us up in three hours.

A short distance on I spied a big stag rolling around in a wet peat bog. Stags do this during the rutting season because it makes them look bigger and blacker. Lady Jean reached for the binoculars to have a look at what the stag was doing. When she saw it roll onto its back she gasped, as she could see that the stag was urinating all over itself. I asked her if she had ever seen that before and she replied, "No. What's all that about?" I explained, "That's to attract the hinds. It's called stag body deodorant or stag after shave lotion." Then I asked her, "Are you going to shoot it or just admire him peeing all over itself." She proceeded to shoot the stag as he stood up. As we approached the stag she exclaimed, "Wow, that's a bit ripe." I replied, "Well the hinds don't mind the smell as it's like a tracking device to let them know where the stag is if they are in need of his services."

115

I decided this was the perfect time to tell her my joke about the two hinds, one of which had just come into season and said to the other, "Have you seen big Staggy today?" The other one said, "No, I haven't seen him, but if you go over in that direction staying downwind you will soon find him. I think he has over done the body lotion this morning." That got Lady Jean roaring with laughter, taking her mind off being sad at having to shoot the two stags that were locked together to laughing at the stag that got himself all titillated up for the hinds ... then she shot him.

I said, "Milady, do you realise that I just ripped open the stag's belly to remove its guts and my sleeve came in contact with its urinated belly, now I'm about to eat my packed lunch with this awful smell hanging around." She just laughed.

Laggan Challenge

As no guests were scheduled, Howard decided we should take two student and go shoot stags around the inaccessible Laggan Cottage area at the base of a hill close to the Newton shore. The two students went with Howard in the Haflinger. They drove north to the top of the Boguillie Road where Howard turned right and crossed over the land to the hill above the old cottage, then they proceeded on foot to hunt for deer. I drove the Land Rover to Sannox Pier to pick up Lady Jean's 12-foot motorboat, then made my way north by sea around the Cock of Arran to Laggan Cottage. By the time I arrived at the cottage Howard had already shot two stags and the students had dragged them down the steep hill behind Laggan Cottage to the seashore.

Our next challenge was to drag the stags, weighing around 23 stone (322 pounds), over slippery rocks and load them into the boat. The students set off toward the boat with the first stag. Howard and I followed dragging the second stag over the rocks. (You can't make this up.) As the students struggled to load the first stag into the boat, they ended up falling into the boat along with the stag resulting in one of its antlers piercing a hole in the side of the boat. Howard let out a few choice words. One of the students commented that the hole was above the water level, but that was before the second stag was loaded into the boat and then I had to get in to drive back

117

to the pier. You guessed it - the water started dribbling in as I headed back to Sannox with me hoping the boat wouldn't sink before making it all the way back to the pier.

As Howard was driving passed Sannox House on his way to meet me at the pier, he had a brainwave when he spotted Willie Innes and Neil Drummond, two estate joiners, replacing windows at Sannox House. He stopped to check with Willie to find out if he could do something to patch up the hole in the boat. Howard, Willie and the students were waiting for me when I returned to Sannox Pier. Thankfully, there was only a few inches of water in the boat.

After off-loading the stags into the Halflinger at the pier, we tipped the boat over and Willie proceeded to do an impressive repair job using a plug and some kind of resin he had made up. Howard was hoping to have the boat repaired quickly as he was taking one of Lady Jean's guests out fishing the next day. There was never a dull moment working for Lady Jean, always something different every day.

Satisfied with the boat repair, we drove off to the kennels to prepare the stags for shipment. Lady Jean had left a note at the kennels for Howard to check up on a report of a poacher being spotted in the burn opposite the estate offices. Howard suggested we both go in case the guy got nasty. You'll never guess who the poacher turned out to be? My cousin, Neil Drummond! He had taken advantage of the two gamekeepers being busy with the deer at the kennels, left his job at Sannox House and jumped into his car to go poaching.

Howard dealt with the situation very quickly by asking Neil how many salmon he had snared. Neil answered "Three." Howard responded, "One for Vic, one for me, and have one for yourself. Now be on your way and don't do this again." Nice one Howard! I never found out what he told Lady Jean.

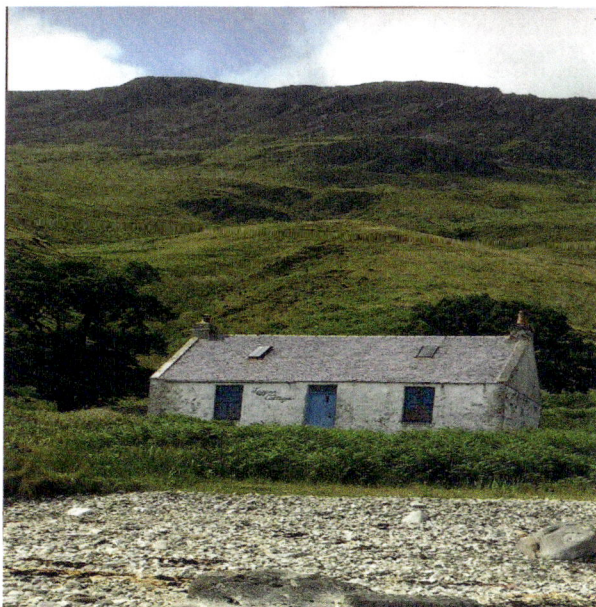

Laggan Cottage - 2 July 2021

119

Tricky Gamekeeper Situation

Howard and I had been instructed to meet with Lady Jean at Strabane House where she provided us with a list of the names and dates of guests that would be visiting Strabame House for the entire shooting season. The guest list read: Lord Polworth, Lord Hornby, Major Henkel, Gardner Green, a Texan oil well owner, and film star Richard Todd.

(By the way, just a little side note and name dropping. Richard Todd had attended Brodick Church with Lady Jean and was kind enough to show me a photograph he had taken from the church balcony during the christening of Alistair Dobson and my daughter, Carol. Sorry for the interruption, a proud dad just wanting to share a special moment. Now back to the story.)

After our meeting she decided we should go over the String Road to the Bridgend Farm area where a burn there marked the boundary between Lady Mary's land to the south and Lady Jean's land to the north. The north end was the best part of the island as that's where most of the deer could be found. At one time there were more deer on the island than people.

As we approached Bridgend Farm, Howard spotted a huge stag with a harem of around ten hinds. He commented that it was going to be a long crawl to reach the herd. I said to Lady Jean, "This is going to be a piece of cake now that you are an expert crawler." (That doesn't sound right does it?) Anyway, off we went with Lady Jean first, then Howard, with me at the rear to avoid bumping into Lady Jean this time.

When we got within shooting distance of the stag, he was on Lady Mary's side but continued to check out the hinds on both sides of the burn for a while. He ended up settling for the hinds on Lady Mary's side. Lady Jean had always told us that she would never shoot a beast that is not on her land. As the stag had taken forever to finally make up his mind and she had run out of patience, she turned to us and whispered, "I'll shoot it where it stands and you two can drag it across to my land."

So that is exactly what we did, then we bled it and removed the guts on her land. If we had gutted it on Lady Mary's land the crows would have given the show away when they swarmed to feed on the entrails. Lady Mary might have noticed this if she happened to be passing on the road. Lady Jean was really chuffed at her days work. Howard left to drive back to Brodick to pick up two young students to come and drag the stag off the hill.

Lady Jean and I sat down to have our packed lunches. She suggested we swap sandwiches. I said, "I've only got cheese. What do you have?" She replied, "Pickled conger eel." Swiftly I answered, "No thanks, Milady." I could see she did not fancy her sandwich choice and asked who had made her sandwich, to which she responded, "It would be Shring and I will Shring his neck when I get home." I commented, "I thought you were going to say that you had made the sandwich."

That's when I told her the joke about Pat & Mick at a building site. When they sat down to have their packed lunch Pat opened his sandwiches and said, "Aww, no cheese again." Mick wanted to know who had made Pat's sandwiches. Pat answered, "I did."

Lady Jean had another fit of laughter so I told her "There will be no more shooting today, Milady, as you are having a fit of the giggles and you just made the gamekeepers feel like poachers today." She responded, "But it was great fun, wasn't it." Another memorable day out on the hills with Lady Jean - she really had such a fantastic sense of humour.

The Old Royal

The first year that Major Henkel came to Arran as Lady Jean's guest was in 1963. He was an avid hunter from Germany. A thin, wiry man who walked with a slight limp. He wore a smart leather jacket, a deerstalker hat with a German insignia on it to cover up a shock of white hair, and he insisted on using his own telescopic rifle. He was a real professional game hunter. Lady Jean prohibited guests from shooting a royal stag because they were to be protected for breeding. Howard and I were well aware of that as she kept reminding us just in case we had forgotten. She was a real stickler for her rules. The major left that year very disappointed that he never had the opportunity to shoot what he called 'a real trophy,' meaning a 12-pointer royal stag.

Major Henkel returned the following year still determined to shoot a royal stag as he wanted to mount the antlers of a royal from Scotland on a wall in his mountain chalet home. If he had two stags to choose from when hunting, he would definitely go for the one that gave him the biggest challenge. Most of the guests left a tip for Howard and me depending on how successful their shooting days had been. When it came to Major Henkel's last day, I was given the job of taking him out shooting.

As the Major, the two students and I were preparing to leave Strabane House, Lady Jean came out to advise us that a switch stag had been seen near the deer gate in Glen Rosa on the left side of the hill. A switch is a stag that has defective antlers with no points. When it fights with another stag, it uses its antlers just like spears giving it a greater advantage to inflict severe damage, therefore, they must be shot to keep them from breeding.

I could see the frown on the Major's face. He was not interested in wasting his time shooting a switch. Anyway, we went to Glen Rosa and he disposed of the switch stag very quickly. The only problem was that the noise from his rifle echoed up the glen and startled all the other deer in the area, so this could turn out to be a long day. And it was.

We eventually came across two stags that had been fighting. One had been badly injured and it so happened that it was a very old royal. You can tell that a stag is getting old when the two bottom tines nearest to its head start to get much smaller and that old stag was as near as the Major was ever going to get for a trophy.

When he crawled into shooting distance, the Major handed me an envelope asking me if he could now have his trophy stag. I quickly opened the envelope and counted £60 ($168.00 based on the 1963 exchange rate). At that time I was earning £6 ($16.80) per week and had never seen that much money before, so I told him he could shoot as many as he liked. He was really pleased with his old royal stag and I could not get home quick enough to show my wife this large amount of money!

A Royal Stag at Lochranza Golf Course - 14 November 2021

Plonker

Howard was having a really bad day. I had worked as Howard's assistant for just over three years and in all that time I never found him anything other than good natured, jovial, and he liked a good laugh. But when it came to handling guns, he was exceptionally strict.

Gardner Green, a tall, brash, heavy set, ruddy complexioned man was scheduled to go fishing and deer hunting with Howard before returning to the USA the next day. Travelling with Gardner Green was his strange mate, a short, heavy set, balding man, with a very nasal voice who I will call Plonker. The name Plonker was very apt as this man should never have been allowed out on the hills with a pop gun never mind a powerful rifle. Neither of the two men struck me as the outdoor type at all.

In the morning I had accompanied Charles to the top of the String Road where he successfully shot a stag. After doing that, I picked up two students and drove to Sannox to meet up with Howard and his guests in the afternoon to go stag hunting.

As we sat at the Sannox Pier eating our lunches, Howard took me aside to tell me what had happened when they were fishing. He went on to say that they had just started fishing when Plonker announced he wanted to go to the bathroom. Howard handed him the mobile boat toilet which was a tin can and Plonker whined, "No, I need to

126

go to the bathroom." Swearing under his breath, Howard pulled up the anchor and the fishing lines and headed the boat for the shore. Luckily for Plonker, Howard always kept the keys to the remote Laggan Cottage and outhouse in his pocket. When they went back out to sea, only two fish were caught and it was Howard that caught them. That was disaster number one. Worse was to come.

After lunch we all went deer hunting. Unbeknown to us, Gardner Green had asked Lady Jean if his mate could have a chance at shooting a stag and she had given him permission. Howard was upset when Gardner told him this and decided we would go up Glen Sannox toward the Devil's Punchbowl area. Climbing toward the mountain we could hear the stags' challenging roars.

On our way up the mountain Plonker wanted to know why it was called the Devil's Punchbowl? Wanting to think up something quick and to lay it on thick, I told him that there's a story going around that the Devil's face had been seen there recently. If he was nervous before, he was a lot worse after hearing that. Plonker was carrying the Duchess of Montrose's Mauser rifle, the equivalent of a 303 and when Howard spoke to him, he turned around pointing the rifle directly at Howard. Howard brusquely shouted, "Don't point that rifle at me!" And then he made an even bigger mistake by doing it a second time. All this happened before Plonker had the opportunity to shoot a stag.

When we were within shooting range of two stags that were fighting, Howard advised Plonker to crawl forward while he positioned himself behind a big rock. The students and I hunkered down behind rocks, staying well behind them. Howard signaled for Plonker to shoot the stag on the right but just then a third stag suddenly appeared seeing an opportunity for him to steal the hinds roaming in the area for himself. The only problem was that the new stag was in between Plonker and Howard.

Plonker happened to turn around and saw the third stag behind him, he panicked, jumped up and ran down the hill shouting, "The biggest thing I have ever shot was a wild turkey!" All the deer in the area scattered and ran away. Howard took off in hot pursuit of Plonker as he was concerned about the safety of the Duchess' rifle being in the hands of such an amateur. Howard had a few choice words with Gardner Green regarding his guest and a bad day just got worse - no stags were shot.

On our return to Strabane House we were greeted by Lady Jean and she inquired, "How was your day boys?" Howard was so upset about the incident that he tore into her for allowing this inexperienced guest to go shooting without first confirming his game hunting background. I don't believe Gardner Green and his mate were ever invited back.

Devil's Punchbowl - 2 July 2021

Albert's New Experience

Lady Jean received a complaint from a farmer in Lochranza that a marauding stag was eating his crops and she wanted me to go over first thing in the morning to deal with it. I was to take her son with me to shoot the stag. My brother was on holiday and staying at my parents house in Brodick. Albert decided he would like to come with us to Lochranza as it would be quite a new experience for him from being a professional golfer in Canada.

I picked Albert up at dawn and we drove to Strabane House to pick up Charles who brought along his black Labrador. When we reached the farm, the farmer let us know we were too late, the stag had left. "You were supposed to be here first thing in the morning." This was at 7:00 a.m. and just getting light.

We decided to cross to the Newton side of the valley so that we could look above the Balarrie Farm to see if the stag was still around. He could not be that far away. Sure enough, he was up on the flat so we crossed over and headed up the hill. Albert was given the job of taking care of the dog. As Charles was getting ready to shoot the stag, I advised my brother to keep a tight hold on the dog and stay down in the heather. He did manage to do that until Charles shot the stag. As soon as the stag was shot, I turned around to see Albert being dragged through the heather by the dog.

The stag was definitely the culprit as its stomach was full of the farmer's turnips. It was a very cold morning and I was happy to be warming my hands in the stag's warm innards. I offered Albert the opportunity to warm his hands, but he declined. He did not look very well after observing the stag being gutted never mind touching it. The guts were scattered for the hooded crows to devour.

The three of us set about dragging the stag down the hill with the dog pulling at the ropes as if he was trying to help us. We headed back to Strabane House with Charles and his dog then my brother and I drove on to the kennels where I skinned and prepared the stag for shipment.

Lady Jean was so pleased with the result of our shoot and, as I had been up since 5:00 a.m., she gave me the rest of the day off. Albert and I borrowed John Basford's boat and spent the rest of the day successfully catching fish off Strabane shore.

White Stag

Lady Jean made up her mind to go deer hunting in North Glen Sannox, which I thought was strange. She had never gone shooting there in the last three years that I was aware of, as she was very superstitious about the area. Another strange thing that we did not do that day was to pick up the two students that would normally accompany us on a deer shoot. This day continued to get stranger, in fact it became a bit creepy.

We arrived at the old North Glen Sannox Village ruins, where Lady Jean's great-great-grandfather, Alexander Douglas Hamilton, 10th Duke of Hamilton (1767-1852), had removed crofter families from the glen to make way for sheep farming during the 1829 clearance. Lady Jean scanned the area with her binoculars and selected a stag right above the old village in the area called The Fort. I drove the Haflinger as far as I could up the steep slope to where the stag was attending to his harem. Lady Jean grabbed her rifle and we set off on foot. Coincidentally, she had her mother's Mauser rifle with her - by this time I was wondering, "What's next?"

We crawled along a ditch to get closer to the stag. One other strange thing, she had not consulted with me if this was the right stag to shoot ... she was determined to shoot this one. The next event was uncanny, even for me and I am not superstitious in any way. As she was about to pull the trigger, a white stag appeared right behind the red stag she was about to shoot. She started to shake. I asked, "What's wrong?" She did not answer, just slowly put the rifle down on the ground then turned to me and said, "Victor take me home." I picked up her rifle and followed her down the hill to the Haflinger. All I could think about in that moment was the local legend about a mysterious white stag that would appear on Arran, forewarning when the head of the Hamilton Clan is close to death or had died.

We drove back to Strabane House, then I met with Howard on his return from deer hunting with guests at the top of the Boguillie Road. He wanted to know where we had been shooting today and I answered, "North Glen Sannox." He stated, "That's against her rules in case there is an accident as we were shooting in the same area."

I suggested he better have a word with her because, "I had just driven her from Glen Sannox to Strabane House and she never spoke a word, then I had watched her pour herself a big glass of brandy. After the shock of seeing the white deer appearing on the hill and knowing the legendary link it has to her family, she might have seen a ghost." His response was, "Aye, right."

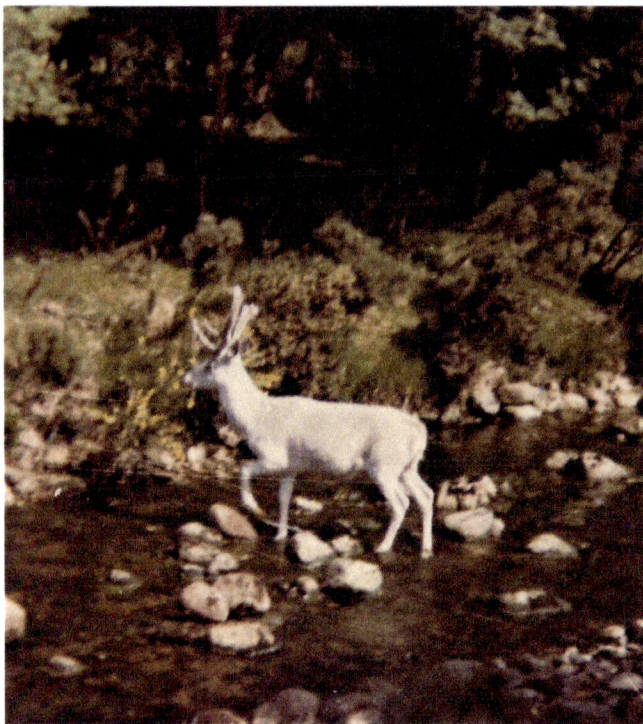

White stag photo from Aunt Elsie's collection N/D

North Glen Sannox Clearance

This story is about the North Glen Sannox clearance as it was told to me by Lady Jean. Her great-great-grandfather, The 10th Duke of Hamilton (1767-1852), was a very keen game hunter with many game hunting friends living on mainland estates that would be invited to visit the castle for the grouse and deer seasons. The Duke's favourite place for shooting game was North Glen Sannox where a community of crofter families lived. The foundations of a few of the ruined cottages are still noticeable to this day.

The Duke advised the crofters in the village that they would have to move as he was planning to use this whole area for sheep farming and game hunting, therefore, they could no longer live there with their families. He agreed to pay half of the fares for families that were willing to emigrate to Canada. On 25 April 1829, 86 islanders (men, women, and children) boarded the brig *Caledonia* in Lamlash to sail to a new life in Canada.

The evicted families that chose to stay on the island were informed they would be required to relocate to the Corrie shore where they would have to build their own cottages and become fishermen as a means to support their families.

It just so happened my great-great-grandfather, Francis Logan, was impacted by the North Glen Sannox clearance. He and his family decided to stay in Corrie and built their own cottage with stones from the shore and the surrounding area. The cottage was named Cliff Cottage.

North Glen Sannox Clearance Ruins - 14 June 2022

Murder on Goatfell

Recalling how my Great-great-grandfather Logan, was forced to move his family to the Corrie shore during the North Glen Sannox clearance reminded me about the murder that was committed on Goatfell in 1889 and the part my great-uncle, Francis (Frank) Logan, had in searching for the lost tourist.

Edwin Rose was a friendly young man from London, England, that became acquainted with John Watson Laurie (of dubious character and travelling under the assumed name of John Annandale) from Coatbridge, Scotland. They met on the steamer-boat, *Ivanhoe*, on a day trip over to Arran during the Glasgow Fair holiday. The two men decided to return to the island on 15 July 1889 to climb Goatfell. Several days later when Edwin did not return to his home in England, he was reported missing.

My great-uncle Frank and his dog participated in the Arran police search party looking for Edwin Rose in the Goatfell area where he had last been seen. During the police investigation climbers confirmed they had seen the two men making the trip up to the top of the mountain on 15 July. Laurie was reported as being seen alone in the Glen Sannox area by other people and also identified by the landlord at the Corrie Hotel. Laurie had actually spoken with the landlord when he had stopped in for a drink before taking on the long walk back to Brodick Village.

On 4 August 1889 my Great-uncle Frank and his dog discovered Rose's battered body concealed under a large boulder in an area between the foot of Goatfell and High Corrie. Edwin was buried in the quaint Sannox Cemetery where a large granite boulder marks his grave. John Watson Laurie was found guilty of murdering Edwin Rose. He was sentenced to hang but his legal team claimed he was insane and he was granted a last-minute reprieve. He was then sentenced to life imprisonment and died in the Perth prison asylum in 1930 at the age of sixty-nine.

Great-uncle Frank told Albert, cousins, Joyce and Neil Drummond, and me all about his dog finding the murdered man on Goatfell when we were children. Great-uncle Frank died in 1949 and is buried with his parents, Robert Logan and Mary Crawford as well as his two sisters in the oldest part of the Sannox graveyard, just a few yards away from Edwin Rose's gravestone. The formidable Devil's Punchbowl Mountain range looms in the background behind the cemetery.

Great-uncle Frank Logan standing outside Cliff Cottage N/D

Edwin Rose's headstone - 14 November 2021

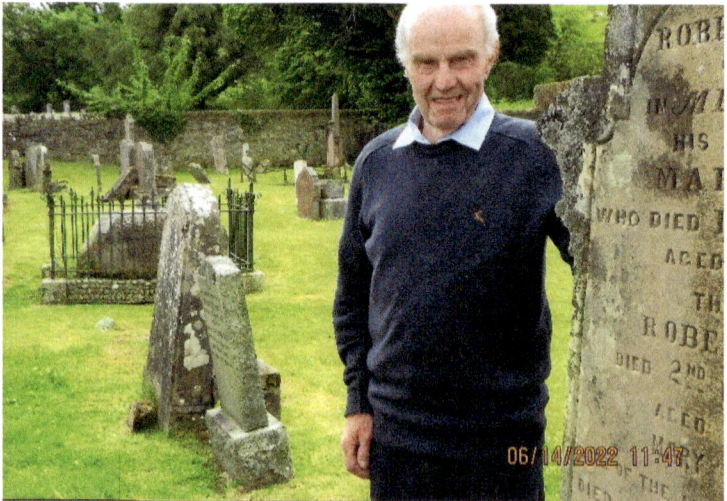

I am standing beside the Logan family gravestone. Edwin Rose's fenced in gravestone can be seen in the background - 14 June 2022

140

On Your Head Be It!

This day of shooting was anything but fun … this was serious stuff. I had been sent to Brodick Pier to pick up Lord Hornby. We had never met but when I caught site of someone in the crowd coming off the ferry wearing a deer stalking hat with a long pheasant feather that stuck out above everyone else, it seemed likely this was my shooting guest. He was a very posh elderly gentleman fashionably dressed in his tweed jacket, plus fours, a bow tie, and wearing a monocle.

Because the first Arran ferry was running late that morning, Lord Hornby asked if he could skip going to the target area to save time as he was returning to the mainland on the evening ferry. To put you in the picture, Lady Jean had a rule that guest shooters were required to stop at the castle drive site where a metal hind was used for target practice. This was to test the sights on the guest's rifle as a precaution to ensure nothing was altered in transit. He did not want to do this, so I told him, "On your head be it!"

We headed to the top of the String Road and came across two stags. One was huge with a very narrow set of antlers, which is not a good trait for breeding. Antlers need to be shaped like a wine glass. Instructing him to shoot that one, I observed him take the shot through the binoculars. If it was shot through the neck, the stag would drop like a stone. If it was shot through the shoulder or heart, it would take off and run for a short distance then drop. But this stag did neither. Lord Hornby had wounded the stag in the shoulder. On checking his rifle, I realised that in spite of him being a repeat deer hunter, this rifle was useless for bringing down a stag. I threw his rifle back to him and told him that had he gone to the castle firing range I would have been able to evaluate the rifle as being unfit for stag hunting. Reluctantly, I gave him the Duchess' powerful Mauser rifle that I had with me.

As we chased after the stag, I could hear Lady Jean's voice in my ear warning me that we were NEVER to leave a wounded animal out on the hill. If you do, she had said, "I will shoot you." Funny how things stick in your mind. Eventually, we did get within shooting range but Lord Hornby was shaking so much from exhaustion that I retrieved the Mauser rifle from him and shot the stag myself. I wasn't taking any more chances as daylight was beginning to fade. The stag was gutted and flagged for the students to locate and remove it off the hill the next day.

As we were returning to the deer gate in Glen Rosa, Howard and two students met up with us. When we reached the deer gate, Lady Jean was waiting for us wanting to know what had kept us as Lord Hornby had missed the last Arran ferry. All I said was, "Ask him."

A year after I had moved away from the Isle of Arran to go to work on the mainland for Shell & BP as a tanker driver at the Ardrossan Depot in November 1965; Lady Jean stopped into Pellegrini's Cafe to buy cigarettes and while chatting with my dad she said, "Tell Victor the stag Lord Hornby shot was the heaviest stag shot in Scotland last year. "Aye, and it was me that shot the bloody thing!

Chapter 6 - AFTER LEAVING ARRAN

Ten Years Later

Ten years after moving away from Arran, I returned with my family during the October school holiday. We had walked along to the Fallen Rocks area where a massive rock pile had slid down the hill to the water's edge on Sannox shore a long time ago. On returning to the car park across from the road up to the Sannox Cemetery my son, Russell, looked up at the Devil's Punchbowl and shouted to me, "Is that the Devil's face and horns showing up on the mountain?" I replied, "That's the best I have ever seen it."

To get a better view of the image we all walked further along the road towards the old rails that crossed over the road. Years ago the rail carriages used to carry barytes from the mines in Glen Sannox to a ship docked at the old Sannox Pier for transportation to the mainland to be crushed and made into paint.

We were standing in the middle of the road looking up at the Devil's facial image that had become visible on the mountain when Lady Jean happened to be driving by. She stopped her car to ask Russell what he was doing standing in the middle of the road. He pointed to the image of the Devil's face appearing on the mountain and she was truly amazed. She recognised me and commented, "I have lived here all my life and this is the first time I have ever seen such a sight." She wanted to know if she had time to go home to Strabane House for her camera. I told her, "No." because the sun was going down and the image would be gone before she returned. It was good to see her again and we had a nice chat.

Can you see the outline of the Devil's face appearing on the mountain behind Aunt Elsie as the sun sets? N/D

Fond Memories

The stories in this book are about all that I can remember of the good old days of being brought up on the picturesque Isle of Arran. Someday, I may consider returning to live there as many others have done before me. When I think about my time at Brodick Primary School and the day Mr. Brodie told me, "You'll never get anywhere in this world" because I had copied Rosemary's test paper; well, it did make an impression on me. I did take it to heart and did okay for myself. Thank you, Mr. Brodie, for your wise words.

In 1976 I was a participant on the Executive Committee for Shell Aviation for the whole of Great Britain and Gibraltar, representing all the airport workers for wages, terms, conditions, and pensions. When Shell and BP were splitting up, I was a Shell Senior Aircraft Fueler attending a high-profile meeting in London and met a young woman, Miss Murchie, who was representing BP. She was a highflier for sure and came from Shiskine. When she saw my name plate, she asked if I was related to Willie Southgate, the Shiskine postman. I told her he was my uncle. I would love to know how she got on at BP. It was hard to believe the two of us came from that small island and here we were representing two of the world's biggest oil companies.

One of my greatest experiences in life was working for Lady Jean at the Home Farm. Writing about the fun and adventures we had together game hunting brought back fond memories of family, friendships, and growing up on Arran. It was an honour and a privilege to have had her as my employer and to have known her as a great friend.

Lady Jean [1920-2017] lived a long and productive life on her beloved Isle of Arran until her death on 13 October 2017, less than one month before her 97th birthday. I did go over to Arran for her funeral service at Brodick Church and also attended the gathering at Stabane House for guests and locals to memorialize her life. She truly was a great lady. The Democrat-Dumbartonshire's Digital Newspaper reported on 13 November 2017 that a white stag was sighted on the island a few days before she passed away.

Family members and friends were influential in encouraging me to write this book about growing up on Arran as a lot of the opportunities for the adventures I had experienced no longer exist. Arran has very few working farms left on the island producing milk now. Brodick Village children can no longer experience the thrill of riding along with John (Toorie) Currie as he made milk deliveries around Brodick in his horse-drawn two-wheeled cart hitched to Jock, the horse. Toorie and his brother, Willie, milked their cows by hand in the 1950s. Corrie no longer has Sandy Watson making his milk deliveries in a horse-drawn cart. The horses came to know all the stops along their route and where they were likely to get a carrot snack. Horses no longer plough farm fields, pull reapers to cut down hay or pull logs down to the Cladach sawmill. Farm cows are no longer milked by hand. Modern farm equipment replaced most of the back breaking manual labour that used to be performed at the Home Farm and other farms. But "Oh, the fun we had then and the memories are extraordinary!"

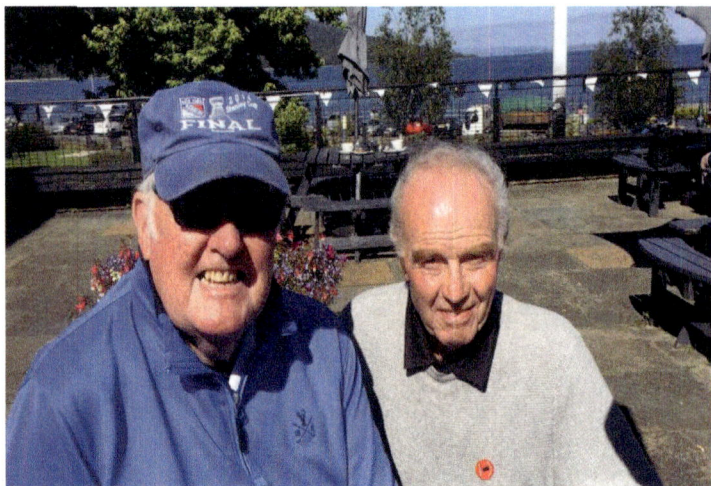

Hacky Hartley and I are still pals in our 80s. Here we are reminiscing at the Douglas Hotel in Brodick on 31 August 2022

Chapter 7 - CHANCE MEETING

Glasgow Excursion

As I was crossing a street in Glasgow on 27 April 2022 on my way to meet with my retired Shell Oil workmates for our monthly luncheon get together, I recognised Charles Fforde walking briskly toward me. I called out to him and we proceeded to have a great time reminiscing about the Home Farm, people we had known like Howard Walker, Major Henkel, Garner Green, and the unforgettable Bob McIntyre. He recalled the time my brother accompanied us deer hunting in Lochranza, the successful Brodick Bay fishing contest we had participated in together, and we had a good laugh about the way too big khaki outfit Lady Jean had supplied me with for deer stalking.

Charles had read the stories I had posted on the Arran Auld Photos website and expressed his delight about the complimentary way I spoke about his mother and that he was looking forward to reading more stories in my book.

On account of the cold air funneling down the street we stepped into a travel agents office to borrow a pen and paper to exchange email addresses and then we decided to stay inside to continue our chat in the warm office. We enjoyed our chance meeting in Glasgow, agreed to stay in touch with each other, then Charles went off to meet his wife for lunch and I continued on to the Society Rooms Restaurant to meet my old pals.

I am blessed to be able to acknowledge this beautiful island as the place of my birth and will be forever grateful for all the people I knew and continue to know there today.

BIBLIOGRAPHY

Chapter 1 - FAMILY TIES

Smith, K. "The Scottish Field - Ten Fascinating Facts about...Arran" Edinburgh, Scotland 15 August 2019 (Scotland in Miniature)

undiscoveredscotland.co.uk. "Brodick Castle & Gardens Feature Page on Undiscovered Scotland;" Livingston, West Lothian, Scotland 2000-2022 (Brodick Castle; William Douglas-Hamilton, 12th Duke of Hamilton [1845-1895])

Beattie, Sarah. Curator, Ayrshire & Arran / Dumfries & Galloway. Mary, Duchess of Montrose [1884-1957], nee Douglas-Hamilton. National Trust for Scotland, nts.org.uk, Scotland 24 June 2021

en.wikipedia.org, WikipediA - The Free Encyclopedia; James Graham, 6th Duke of Montrose [1878-1954], N/D

Chapter 2 - GROWING UP ON ARRAN

Jean Glen, Brodick - *A Century of Golf, Brodick Golf Club*, Isle of Arran, Scotland 1997

Bibliography continued:

Chapter 4 - HOME FARM

Davies, Carey. "Country Diary: on the hunt for some of the rarest trees in the world - Isle of Arran, Firth of Clyde." theguardian.com 6 August, 2018 (Whitebeam trees)

Smith, K. "Ten Fascinating Facts about...Arran," Scottish Field, Edinburgh, Scotland 15 August 2019 (Endangered Whitebeams)

en.wikipedia.org. RMS *Queen Elizabeth 2*, N/D (Sea trials performed off the Arran coast)

Chapter 5 - DEER HUNTING

"Obituary - Lady Jean Fforde [1920-2017], Scottish aristocrat, Arran landowner, codebreaker at Bletchley Park." The Herald Scotland, Glasgow, Scotland 18 October 2017

Fforde, Lady Jean, *Feet on the Ground - from Castles to Catastrophe*. Stuart Titles Ltd., Glasgow, Scotland 2001 (Mysterious white deer)

Bibliography continued:

MacKenzie, W. M. *The Book of Arran Vol 2.* The Arran Society of Glasgow, Hugh Hopkins: Glasgow, Scotland 1914 (Alexander Douglas-Hamilton, 10th Duke of Hamilton [1767-1852] and the North Sannox Clearance).

Hamilton, J. *Scottish Murders* Geddes & Grosset, David Dale House; New Lanark Scotland Reprinted 2002 (Death on Goatfell)

Chapter 6 - AFTER LEAVING ARRAN

Heaney, B. "Death Announcement: Lady Jean Graham Sibyl Violet Graham Fforde." The Democrat - Dumbartonshire's Digital Newspaper Dumbarton, Scotland 13 November 2017 (Mysterious white stag sited on Arran)

GLOSSARY

blether	chat or conversation
bothy	cottage
bunk	hurried departure or escape
burn	stream or brook
chanty pot	bed pan/chamber pot
clearances	removal of people from land to free it for alternative uses
coo pats	cow manure
crofter	small rented farm
death duties	taxes
dreep	drip
factor	estate manager
faither	father
fisty cuff	fight with bare knuckles
guddle	catching fish with your hands
highland fling	Scottish dance
hooses	house

GLOSSARY continued:

kent	known
knackered	very tired; exhausted
lorry	truck
mangle	hand wringer used to squeeze water out of clothes & linens
messages	shopping
midges	small two-winged biting fly found near marshes
nicked	helped ourselves
nicky-tams	straps or string tied around the leg below the knee to raise trousers above the level of farmyard dirt
plonker	unskilled
smiddy	blacksmith/farrier
snookered	left in a difficult position
toby jug	beer jug/mug of man wearing a three-cornered hat
tousled	untidy hair
trap	a light, two wheeled carriage pulled by a pony or horse
wean	a young child

ABOUT THE AUTHOR

Victor Southgate was born and grew up on the Isle of Arran, Scotland. He now resides in Kirkintilloch, Scotland.

Printed in Great Britain
by Amazon

24454545R10089